history

# American History A
## Student Guide

Semester 1

**Illustrations Credits**

All illustrations © K12 Inc. unless otherwise noted

**About K12 Inc.**

K12 Inc., a technology-based education company, is the nation's leading provider of proprietary curriculum and online education programs to students in grades K–12. K12 provides its curriculum and academic services to online schools, traditional classrooms, blended school programs, and directly to families. K12 Inc. also operates the K12 International Academy, an accredited, diploma-granting online private school serving students worldwide. K12's mission is to provide any child the curriculum and tools to maximize success in life, regardless of geographic, financial, or demographic circumstances. K12 Inc. is accredited by CITA. More information can be found at www.K12.com.

978-1-60153-199-5

Printed by RR Donnelley, Kendallville, IN, USA, May 2016

# Table of Contents

## Unit 4: Thirteen Colonies, Part 2

## Unit 5: Road to Revolution

## Unit 6: The American Revolution

## Unit 7: The Constitution

# Student Guides, Worksheets, and Assessments

# Student Guide
## Lesson 1: History and *A History of US*

Early Native Americans were as different from one another as any of us are today, but they shared a common respect for nature and the land. Study the physical geography of North America and how it affected their lives. Learn how the first Americans reached this continent, and explore the rich diversity of Native American cultures before European contact.

The history of the United States is the history of every American. It's your history, your story. It's a story people all over the world want to study. It's not like the history of any other place. Americans don't share the same race or religion. We don't all speak the same language. Some American families have been Americans for centuries. Others became Americans last week. Americans are very different from one another. But we all share a belief in democracy. And that makes us one.

## Lesson Objectives
- Describe the format and features of the text, including its theme, structure, use of primary sources, and additional information in the margins.
- Identify at least two reasons Joy Hakim gives for studying American history.

---

# PREPARE

Approximate lesson time is 60 minutes.

## Advance Preparation
- View the Introduction to American History A, located in the first lesson.

## Materials
For the Student

    📖 A History Of Us

    📖 Getting Started

    A History of US (Concise Edition), Volume A (Prehistory to 1800) by Joy Hakim

    History Journal

---

# LEARN
## Activity 1: Introducing American History A *(Offline)*

### Instructions
**Getting Started**

The book you are about to begin is full of stories. It has pictures and drawings and even some cartoons. But it is different from many storybooks because its stories are all true. The author, Joy Hakim, is a wonderful storyteller. Every one of her stories has something to do with you. How can that be? Chapter 1 will explain.

---

- First, look at the cover of *A History of US (Concise Edition),* Volume A (Prehistory to 1800). It is the first book in a series called *A History of US*. There are four books in all, but you'll use only two this year.
- The first volume covers prehistory to 1800. Prehistory is all the things that happened before people could write. And who were the first Americans? This first volume will tell you that story.
- Answer the first eight questions on the Getting Started sheet.

You did some detective work to answer those questions. Historians do a lot of detective work to find facts and think about what they find. The thinking you just did about the picture is called *document analysis*. You'll do more of that, but for now, let's get back to detective work.

- Answer the rest of the questions on the Getting Started sheet.
- Check your answers with an adult.
- Put the activity sheet in your History Journal.

Do you know what a *primary source document* is? *Primary* means that it is original, actually from the time and place where something happened. A *document* is anything that is on paper (or something like paper). It could be a deed, a will, a letter, a painting, or a photograph. Even a film taken while something happened is a primary source. So are other things, but they are always from the time and place of the event.

You will see many primary sources in *A History of US*. You'll find definitions, explanations, and extra information, too. Look at those before or after you read the text, or you'll miss things you'll want to know. Now, it's time to get started. Do you know why people study history? There are many reasons. The author, Joy Hakim, will tell you why she thinks history is important. See if you agree.

**Read**

Stories of the first Americans, of those who came from Europe, Africa, and Asia centuries ago, and of some who came last week are all part of your story. America's story is fascinating—with no end yet. But that's not the only reason to learn it. Chapter 1, "History? Why?" explains.

Read Chapter 1, pages 2–6, and do the following:

- Make a list of reasons for studying American history in your History Journal.
- Complete the History of US sheet.

Vocabulary

Look for the following terms as your read and write a definition for each term in your History Journal.

- democracy
- liberty
- justice

## About Your History Journal

The History Journal is a three-ring binder with loose-leaf paper. You will do a lot of writing in your journal this year. You'll also use it to keep the pages that you print from the History lessons. Punch holes in these pages and insert them in order in the History Journal. Set aside a section of the journal for vocabulary. When you are asked to define terms as you read, you will put them in that special section. The journal will be a valuable study guide for you.

Name _____     Date _____

## Getting Started

You'll need to become a detective to find the right answers for all the questions below. Get ready to search for the answers. They are all in *A History of US* (Concise Edition), Volume A (Prehistory to 1800).

1. Look at the front cover of the book. Who is the author of *A History of US*?

   _____

2. Who do you think the person shown on the front cover is? _____

   _____ What things in the picture helped you decide?

   _____

3. What time period does this volume of *A History of US* cover? _____

4. Look at the table of contents. Into how many parts is this book divided? _____

5. What is the title of Chapter 26, and on what page does it begin? _____

6. Look at pages 434 and 435. What is a collection of maps called? _____ Name

   a mountain range located in North America. _____

7. On what page does the glossary begin? _____ What is the definition of *democracy*?

   _____

8. Which primary source begins on page 401 of the appendix of primary sources?

   _____

Turn to Chapter 59, which begins on page 276.

9. What is the title of this Chapter? _____

When you read a chapter, make sure you take a look at all of the images. You may see images of paintings, drawings, prints, illustrations, photographs, documents, and other primary or secondary sources. Take a moment to study each image and read its caption.

10. Who is shown in the painting on page 276? _____

    How did this man earn a living? _____

Sidebars are a common element of the chapters in this book. They are located in the margins and are set off from the rest of the text with red lines. Sidebars provide additional information related to the main text.

**11.** What is the connection between the sidebar on page 277 and the main text? _____

_____

_____

Some chapters include a map. Make sure you read the caption and study the map.

**12.** In which two towns were battles fought? _____

Sometimes words from the text will be defined in the margns. These keywords are set off from the rest of the text with yellow lines.

**13.** Look at the keyword on page 281. What are *regulars*? _____

Some chapters have a special feature. Look at page 282 to see what a feature looks like.

**14.** What is this feature about? _____

Name _____  Date _____

## *A History of US*

Can you remember the theme of *A History of US*? Rewrite it by piecing together the following phrases:

| | |
|---|---|
| No other nation in | so much freedom, so |
| that has ever existed. | America is |
| the most remarkable nation | and so much opportunity |
| has ever provided | United States of |
| much justice, | the history of the world, |

We believe that the _____

_____

_____

_____ to so many people.

**Thinking Cap Question!** When Marcus Garvey said, "A man without history is like a tree without roots," he was making an analogy. An analogy is a comparison based on the resemblance between two things. How do you feel about history? Do you think that history is important? Write an analogy that describes what history means to you.

# *Student Guide*
## Lesson 2: Maps and Directions

Do you want to know more about the world? Maps and globes are packed with information. Maps are much easier to store and carry around than globes. But it's really tough to show a round earth on flat paper, so all maps are slightly distorted.

### Lesson Objectives
- Identify characteristics and uses of maps and globes.
- Explain the reason for distortion on maps and the purpose of projections.
- Identify cardinal and intermediate directions.

---

# PREPARE

Approximate lesson time is 60 minutes.

### Materials
For the Student

Understanding Geography: Map Skills and Our World (Level 5)

History Journal

---

# LEARN
## Activity 1: The Earth on Maps and Globes *(Online)*
### Instructions
- Read Activity 1, "The Earth on Maps and Globes" (pages 4–7), in *Understanding Geography*.
- Answer Questions 1–14 in your History Journal.
- If you have time, you may want to answer the Skill Builder Questions on page 7.
- After you have finished, compare your answers with the ones in the Learning Coach Guide.

---

# ASSESS

## Lesson Assessment: Maps and Directions (*Online*)
You will complete an online assessment covering the main goals of this lesson. Your assessment will be scored by the computer.

---

# Student Guide
## Lesson 3: (Optional) Grids

Imaginary lines of latitude and longitude can help you find any place on earth. Weather forecasters use them to track storms. Rescuers use them to find ships in trouble at sea. They function like a global address. Even though you may skip this lesson, you must complete the **Read On** section before moving on to the next lesson.

### Lesson Objectives
- Identify *latitude, longitude, absolute location,* and *hemisphere.*
- Use longitude and latitude to determine absolute location.
- Use maps and globes to locate places.

---

# PREPARE

Approximate lesson time is 60 minutes.

### Materials
For the Student

Understanding Geography: Map Skills and Our World (Level 5)

History Journal

A History of US (Concise Edition), Volume A (Prehistory to 1800) by Joy Hakim

---

# LEARN
## Activity 1. Optional: Latitude and Longitude *(Online)*
### Instructions
- Read Activity 2, "The Coordinate System: Latitude and Longitude" (pages 8–11), in *Understanding Geography*.
- Answer Questions 1–15 in your History Journal.
- If you have time, you may want to answer the Skill Builder Questions on page 11.
- After you have finished, compare your answers with the ones in the Learning Coach Guide.

## Activity 2. Optional: Chapters 2 and 3 *(Online)*
### Instructions
During the Ice Age, land bridges promoted the movement of people and animals into new regions.

We think the Eskimos are the descendants of the last ancient Asians to reach North America. These people actually call themselves by a different name: the Inuit. They live in Alaska, Greenland, Siberia, and northern Canada. These areas are all part of the icy far North.

---

**Read On**

Read Chapter 2, pages 7–11, and Chapter 3, pages 12–16, in *A History of US (Concise Edition),* Volume A (Prehistory to 1800). As you read, think about what geographic features and conditions helped cause the movement of people into North and South America. Also think about how the Inuit adapted to the harsh environments found there.

Vocabulary

You'll see these terms as you read. Write a brief definition in your History Journal for each term as you come to it.

- Eskimo
- igloo
- Inuit

**Beyond the Lesson**

How do forecasters follow hurricanes? Visit the National Hurricane Center to find out. Learn about history's deadliest hurricanes. Print your own tracking charts and follow the path of a hurricane.

# Activity 3. Optional: Hurricanes *(Online)*

# Student Guide
## Lesson 4: North American Beginnings

The first Americans probably came from Asia. They followed their prey, large mammals, across a land bridge from Asia to North America. That land bridge no longer exists, but their trek thousands of years ago led to the settlement of North and South America.

### Lesson Objectives
- Recognize the role of an archaeologist.
- Locate the Bering Sea and land bridge on a map or globe.
- Trace the migration route of the earliest Americans.
- Describe the reason for migration to the Americas as the need to follow herds for food during the Ice Age.
- Describe and categorize Inuit lands, shelter, food, customs, and beliefs.
- Describe the reasons for migration to the Americas as the need to follow herds for food during the Ice Age.

---

# PREPARE

Approximate lesson time is 60 minutes.

### Materials
For the Student

📖 Discussion Questions

📖 Native American Groups

A History of US (Concise Edition), Volume A (Prehistory to 1800) by Joy Hakim

History Journal

### Keywords and Pronunciation
taiga (TIY-guh)

---

# LEARN
## Activity 1: The First Americans (Offline)
### Instructions
Check Your Reading (Chapter 2, pages 7–11, and Chapter 3, pages 12–16)

- Try to answer all the questions on the Discussion Questions sheet.
- If you have trouble, read that part of Chapter 2 or 3 again.
- Discuss your answers with an adult.

---

### Native American Groups

In this lesson, you will begin adding information to a table to compare Native American groups. Use the table in the Native American Groups sheet to help you organize what you read about the Inuit in Chapter 3. Fill in the row on the Inuit. If you aren't sure how to fill in a section, review the chapter. Ask an adult to check your work. **Keep the Native American Groups sheet in your History Journal so you can add information to it in later lessons.**

### Migration

Do you understand the meaning of the word *migration*? Migration is movement from one area to another. The word has a verb form: *to migrate*.

Here are two definitions of to *migrate*. Both usually apply to large groups of animals or people.

1. To move from one country or place to another
2. To go back and forth from one region or climate to another for feeding or breeding

Why is migration important? Because the "history of us" begins with the migration of human beings from Asia to the Americas. Later, there will be other important migrations as well.

Go back online and click "From Asia to the Americas." Trace the migration route of the earliest Americans.

### Assessment

Stay online to complete your assessment.

---

# ASSESS
## Lesson Assessment: North American Beginnings (*Online*)
You will complete an online assessment covering the main goals of this lesson. Your assessment will be scored by the computer.

Name _____          Date _____

## Discussion Questions

Trace the migration route of the earliest Americans on a globe. To see if you traced the correct route, look at the map in Chapter 2.

Now answer the following questions. Make sure you've read Chapters 2 and 3.

1.  Why did people leave Asia and migrate to the Americas?

     _____

     _____

2.  What is an archaeologist?

     _____

     _____

3.  Why was America a "hunter's heaven"?

     _____

     _____

     _____

4.  At the end of the Ice Age, what happened to North America's glaciers and seas?

     _____

     _____

5.  What happened to the land bridge connecting Asia and North America?

     _____

     _____

6. Where did the name *Indians* come from?

_____

_____

_____

7. What things did the first Americans do well? What did they invent? What did they make?

_____

_____

_____

_____

_____

8. How did the horse affect Indian hunting?

_____

_____

9. Where do Eskimos (the Inuit) live today?

_____

_____

Name _____    Date _____

## Native American Groups

Use this graphic organizer to help you gather, organize, and display facts and concepts from Unit 1.

| | Economic Activities | Location | Customs/ Beliefs | Food | Shelter |
|---|---|---|---|---|---|
| Inuit | | | | | |
| Anasazi | | | | | |
| Indians of the Northwest | | | | | |
| Plains Indians | | | | | |
| Mound Builders | | | | | |
| Eastern Woodland Indians | | | | | |

# Student Guide
## Lesson 5: Cliff Dwellers

In Europe, people were building castles and going on crusades. At about the same time, the Anasazi were living in the southwestern United States. The Anasazi were farmers in a desert area. They are gone now, but they left stone ruins that give us clues about their lives.

### Lesson Objectives

- Describe the Anasazi as cliff dwellers.
- Locate on a map the area where the cliff dwellers lived.
- Describe Anasazi shelter, food, customs, and beliefs.
- Describe the hardships of farming in a desert region.
- Identify Pueblo peoples as the Anasazi's modern descendants.

---

# PREPARE

Approximate lesson time is 60 minutes.

### Materials

For the Student

A History of US (Concise Edition), Volume A (Prehistory to 1800) by Joy Hakim

History Journal

Cliff Dwellers Assessment Sheet

### Keywords and Pronunciation

**prestige** (preh-STEEZH)

---

# LEARN
## Activity 1: Remember the Cliff Dwellers *(Offline)*
### Instructions
### Read

- Read Chapter 4, pages, 17–22. As you read, fill in the row on the Anasazi in your Native American Groups table.
- On a map of the United States, locate the area where the cliff dwellers lived.
- Ask an adult to check your work, and then save the table in your History Journal.

---

Vocabulary

You'll see these terms as you read. Write a brief definition for each term as you come to it.

- adobe (uh-DOH-bee)
- Anasazi (ah-nuh-SAH-zee)
- drought (drowt)
- mesa (MAY-suh)
- pueblo (PWEH-bloh)

## Review

Review what you have learned about the Anasazi using the flash cards online.

## Read On

Has learning about the Anasazi made you hot and dry? Let's go somewhere cooler—the American Northwest, where Washington and Oregon meet the Pacific Ocean. This is where the Indians of the Northwest lived, and still do.

- Read Chapter 5, pages 23–26.
- As you read, look for the information for the North American Groups table.
- Be prepared to say if you'd accept an invitation to a potlatch, and why.

Vocabulary

You'll see these words as you read. Write a brief definition for each as you come to it.

- prestige
- potlatch
- totem pole

# ASSESS

## Lesson Assessment: Cliff Dwellers (*Offline*)

You will complete an offline assessment covering the main goals for the lesson. An adult will score the assessment and enter the results online.

Name _____    Date _____

## Lesson Assessment

1. Who were the Anasazi?

   _____

   _____

   _____

2. Describe Anasazi shelters. In your description, define the word *kiva*.

   _____

   _____

   _____

3. What were Anasazi customs like? What did they believe?

   _____

   _____

   _____

4. The Tiwa, Hopi, and Zuni Indians of the Southwest are some of the Pueblo peoples. What is their relationship to the Anasazi?

   _____

   _____

5. What is a *pueblo*, and what does it have to do with the Anasazi?

   _____

   _____

6. Name two kinds of food the Anasazi grew. Why was farming difficult for them?

   _____

   _____

**7.** Which area on the map did the Anasazi live?

(A) 1

(B) 2

(C) 3

(D) 4

(E) 5

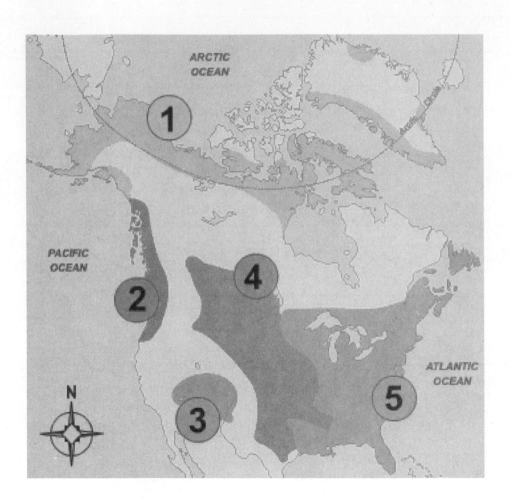

# *Student Guide*
## Lesson 6: Indians of the Northwest

The people of the Pacific Northwest used the ocean, rain, and forest to live well. They formed societies with classes based on wealth and prestige.

### Lesson Objectives

- Locate the area where the Northwest Indians lived on a map.
- Describe Northwest Indian shelter, food, beliefs, and customs, including totem poles.
- Use maps and graphs to locate and describe major climate regions of the United States.
- Analyze photographs to gather information on Indian life in the Pacific Northwest.

# PREPARE

Approximate lesson time is 60 minutes.

## Materials

For the Student

🖳 Document Analysis: Life on the Northwest Coast

A History of US (Concise Edition), Volume A (Prehistory to 1800) by Joy Hakim

Understanding Geography: Map Skills and Our World (Level 5)

History Journal

# LEARN
## Activity 1: Northwest Indians Show Off *(Offline)*
### Instructions
**Check Your Reading (Chapter 5, pages 23–26)**

- Pretend you received an invitation to a potlatch. Tell an adult why you would or would not like to go.
- Complete the row for the Northwest tribes on your Native American Groups table. If you don't know what to write, look for the information in the chapter.
- Keep your table in your History Journal.
- Click Flash Cards to review Chapter 5.

**Use What You Know**

What can you learn from photographs? Probably more than you think. Study some photographs that show life on the Northwest coast.

- Complete the Document Analysis: Life on the Northwest Coast sheet.
- Discuss your work with an adult.

### Climate

Think about the Indians of the American Northwest. The climate there is different from the climates where the Inuit and the Anasazi lived. You can use a climate map to tell what kind of climate different regions of a country or continent have.

- Read Activity 3, "Climate" (pages 12–15), in *Understanding Geography*.
- Answer Questions 1–10 in your History Journal.
- If you have time, you may want to answer the Skill Builder Questions on page 15.
- After you have finished, compare your answers with the ones in the Learning Coach Guide.

### Assessment

Complete the assessment online.

# ASSESS

## Lesson Assessment: Indians of the Northwest (*Online*)

You will complete an online assessment covering the main goals of this lesson. Your assessment will be scored by the computer.

Name _____          Date _____

## Document Analysis: Life on the Northwest Coast

You can learn a lot by studying, or analyzing, documents such as photographs. Document analysis is a skill that historians use to learn about the past.

**Step 1: Observation**

You will analyze four photographs on page 26 of Chapter 5. For each, follow these steps:

1. Study the photograph. Don't just glance at it—really look at it. Form an impression of the whole picture in your mind.

2. Now examine individual objects in the photograph.

3. Divide the photograph into four equal sections, or quadrants. Study each section. Look for details.

4. Complete this chart. List people, objects, and activities you notice in the photograph. You may find there is no information for one or two of the categories.

| Photograph | People | Objects | Activities |
|---|---|---|---|
| 1. mask | | | |
| 2. Haida village | | | |
| 3. Nootka smoking fish | | | |
| 4. Tlingit salmon rattle | | | |

**Step 2: Inference**

Based on your observations, list at least two things you might infer from each photograph. To infer is to draw a conclusion based on facts. For example, if you see smoke from a distance, you could infer that there is a fire.

Photograph 1: mask

1. _____

2. _____

Photograph 2: Haida village

1. _____

2. _____

Photograph 3: Nootka smoking fish

1. _____

2. _____

Photograph 4: carved object

1. _____

2. _____

**Step 3: Questions**

What questions come to mind when you study this photograph? Where could you find the answers to those questions? Select one photograph to ask these questions about.

Photograph: _____

1. What questions come to mind when you study this photograph? _____

_____

_____

2. Where could you find the answers to those questions? _____

_____

_____

# Student Guide
## Lesson 7: Touring the Continent

Take a trip across North America. See the different kinds of land. The Native Americans who live in various states across the country are different, too. In fact, there is no such thing as a "typical" Native American.

## Lesson Objectives

- Demonstrate mastery of important knowledge and skills in this unit.
- Transfer written information on the geography of North America to a map.
- Identify geographic reasons for diversity among Native American groups.
- Recognize that there were hundreds of different Indian peoples, tribes, and languages.
- Locate the Bering Sea and land bridge on a map or globe.
- Describe the reasons for migration to the Americas as the need to follow herds for food during the Ice Age.
- Trace the migration route of the earliest Americans.
- Define the following words: *Eskimo, Inuit, kayak,* and *igloo.*
- Locate the regions where Inuit live on a map.
- Describe and categorize Inuit shelter, food, customs, and beliefs.
- Describe the Anasazi as cliff dwellers.
- Locate on a map the area where the cliff dwellers lived.
- Describe Anasazi shelter, food, customs, and beliefs.
- Locate the area where the Northwest Indians lived on a map.
- Describe Northwest Indian shelter, food, beliefs, and customs, including totem poles.
- Identify Pueblo peoples as the Anasazi's modern descendants.

---

# PREPARE

Approximate lesson time is 60 minutes.

## Materials

For the Student

- Taking a Tour

    A History of US (Concise Edition), Volume A (Prehistory to 1800) by Joy Hakim

    Understanding Geography: Map Skills and Our World (Level 5)

- The Earliest Americans Assessment Sheet

# LEARN
## Activity 1: Take a Tour of North America *(Offline)*

### Instructions
### Read

Try to imagine an Inuit visiting the Anasazi. These two groups lived in very different places with different climates. The Inuit lived—and still live—in the icy far north of North America. The Anasazi lived in the Southwest. Each had different shelters, food, customs, and beliefs.

There are big differences in the land and climate going south to north between the Southwest and the Arctic. There are also big differences going west to east across North America. For centuries, these differences have affected how people live on different parts of the continent.

- Print the Taking a Tour sheet. Notice what it asks you to look for.
- Read Chapter 6, pages 27–33.
- As you read, look at the map on pages 68 and 69 in *Understanding Geography* and follow the journey.
- Follow the instructions on the Taking a Tour sheet. Look at the Thinking Cap Question. What else can you add to your map?

### Mid-Unit Assessment

Ask an adult to print the Mid-Unit Assessment. After you complete the written assessment, an adult will enter the results online.

### Read On

When people first migrated to North America, the region called the Great Plains was a hunter's paradise. But the climate changed, and life on the plains became difficult.

- Read Chapter 7, pages 34–37.
- As you read, think about how the land and climate affected the lives of the Plains Indians.
- Figure out how horses changed everything.

Vocabulary

You'll see these terms as you read. Write a brief definition for each term as you come to it.

- plains
- tepee
- nomad

---

# ASSESS

## Mid-Unit Assessment: The Earliest Americans (*Offline*)

You will complete an offline Mid-Unit Assessment covering the goals for Lessons 4, 5, and 6. An adult will score the assessment and enter the results online.

Name _____     Date _____

## Taking A Tour

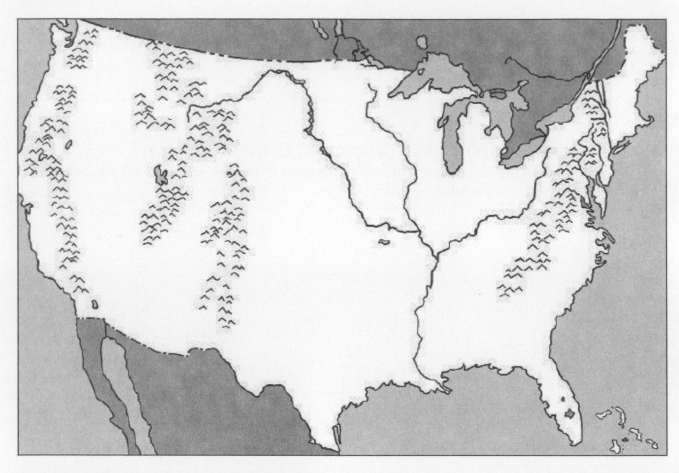

Are you ready for a trip across the United States? As you travel, trace your route and label your stops on the map above. Bon voyage!

1.  You start your journey on the West Coast where the giant redwood trees grow. Label the West Coast on the map.

2.  Travel east over the rugged mountains of California, and over the desert to the Rocky Mountains. Draw and label both mountain chains on the map.

3.  Continue east over grasslands covered with buffalo and prairie dogs to the great river called the Mississippi. Label the river and its two branches, the Missouri River which flows from the west, and the Ohio River from the east.

4.  Still traveling east over thick forests, find the ancient Appalachian Mountains. Label this mountain chain on the map.

5.  Go east and you should be on the Atlantic Coast. Label it.

Adapted from *A History of US*

**Thinking Cap Question!** Turn your map into a picture map of the nation. Add redwoods, cactus, grasslands, and forests where they grow. You can also add animals, such as buffalo, grizzly bears, prairie dogs, and whales. Where does each type of animal live?

Adapted from *A History of US*

Name                                          Date

## Mid-Unit Assessment

**1.** Write the letters for the four items below in their correct places on the map.

    **A.** Northwest Coast Indians

    **B.** Bering Strait

    **C.** Inuit

    **D.** Anasazi

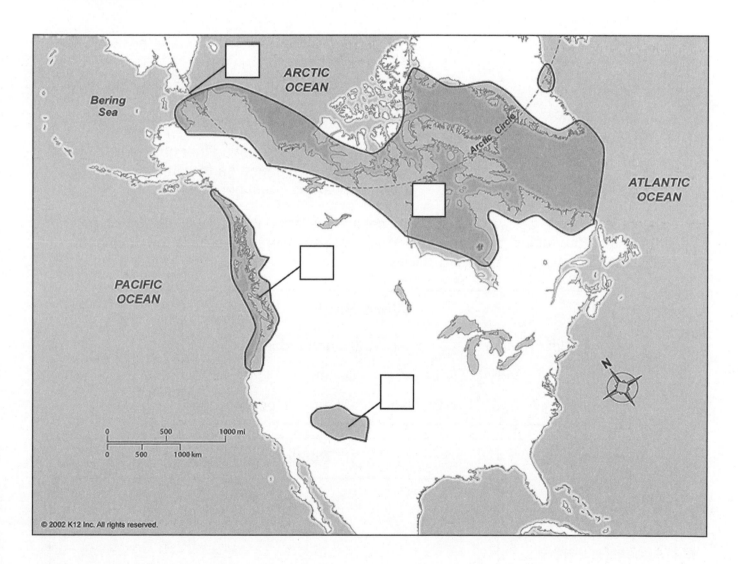

2. Match the terms on the left with their definitions on the right. Write your answers in the blanks.

_____ potlatch

_____ kiva

_____ igloo

_____ Anasazi

_____ totem pole

_____ Inuit

A. a round room dug into the ground where Anasazi gathered to make laws, discuss problems, and hold religious ceremonies

B. animal and human figures carved from fir trees and painted; a symbol of a Northwest Indian family's power and rank

C. a term meaning "ancient enemies," used by Navaho Indians to describe another tribe of Native Americans who lived in the American Southwest

D. a domed house made of snow bricks with ice windows

E. a term meaning "the people," used by the people who live in the far north of North America to describe themselves

F. a party with much feasting that has been planned for years, and ends with the host giving away his finest possessions

3. Complete the table below. In the second column, write the words from the word bank that relate to the Indian peoples listed. You must use all of the words in the word bank, and you should not use any word twice.

| Word Bank |
| --- |
| Cliff dwelling    Valued wealth and property    Tundra |
| Very tall fir trees    Desert    Farmers |
| Adobe    Blubber    Large wooden canoes |

| Indian Peoples | Related Words |
| --- | --- |
| Inuit | |
| Anasazi | |
| Northwest Coast | |

Read each question and its answer choices. Fill in the bubble in front of the word or words that best answer the question.

4. People left Asia to migrate to America during the Ice Age because they followed the animals. The animals and the people were looking for more food.

&#9398; True

&#9399; False

5. When the first Europeans arrived, there were 17 different Indian peoples, tribes, and languages in North America.

&#9398; True

&#9399; False

6. The plants, animals, people, and land in the eastern and western parts of North America are the same.

&#9398; True

&#9399; False

7. How did the first Americans get to North America?

&#9398; They rowed across in canoes from Africa.

&#9399; They walked over a land bridge from Asia.

&#9400; They sailed in ships from Europe.

&#9401; They walked over a land bridge from South America.

8. Which of these peoples believe they are descendants of the Anasazi?

&#9398; Inuit

&#9399; Pueblo

&#9400; Asians

&#9401; Maya

# Student Guide
## Lesson 8: The Plains Indians

In the center of the continent, big game animals began to disappear. This changed the lives of the Native Americans who lived there. They had to adapt to the harsh environment of the prairie. Another big change came into their lives much later. The Spanish brought horses to North America.

### Lesson Objectives

- Identify and describe Plains Indians shelter, food, customs, beliefs, and nomadic way of life.
- Identify different kinds of regions.
- Analyze maps to gain information about regions.
- Describe three changes that occurred as a result of the Spanish introduction of the horse to North America.
- Explain that the Plains Indians depended on the buffalo for food, clothing, shelter, and tools.

# PREPARE

Approximate lesson time is 60 minutes.

### Materials

For the Student

A History of US (Concise Edition), Volume A (Prehistory to 1800) by Joy Hakim

Understanding Geography: Map Skills and Our World (Level 5)

History Journal

# LEARN
## Activity 1: Plains Indians Are Not Plain at All *(Offline)*
### Instructions
Check Your Reading (Chapter 7, pages 34–37)

- Explain to an adult what happened when the Spanish introduced the horse to North America.
- Complete the row for the Plains Indians on your Native American Groups table. If you have trouble, look over Chapter 7 again.
- Go back online and use the Flash Cards to review Chapter 7.
- Stay online and click "On the Plains" to play a game.

**Native American Cultural Regions**

Historians organize tribes of early Native Americans into different cultural regions. Groups of people in each region had similar ways of life. For example, both the Chinook and Yakima tribes lived in the region called the Northwest Coast. These two groups had many things in common. You can use a cultural region map and a vegetation map to find out why.

- Read Activity 14, "Regions" (pages 56–59), in *Understanding Geography*.
- Answer Questions 1–12 in your History Journal.
- If you have time, you may want to answer the Skill Builder Questions on page 59
- After you have finished, compare your answers with the ones in the Learning Coach Guide.

**Read On**

You probably know that the ancient Egyptians built large structures thousands of years ago. They weren't the only people to do that. Did you know that east of the Great Plains, a group of Native Americans were great builders too? They had big cities, well-organized governments, and beautiful art, and they built mounds.

Read Chapter 8, pages 38–41. As you read, figure out:

- Why did the "Mound Builders" make mounds?
- Do any remain?
- What happened to the Mound Builders?

# ASSESS

## Lesson Assessment: The Plains Indians (*Online*)

You will complete an online assessment based on the North American Cultural Regions activity from the lesson. Your assessment will be scored by the computer.

# Student Guide
## Lesson 9: The Mound Builders

The Mound Builders flourished for more than 2,000 years. They built great structures of earth that rivaled the pyramids. Then, like the Anasazi, they faded from history. They left behind unsolved mysteries.

### Lesson Objectives
- Locate the area where the Mound Builders live on a map.
- Describe the findings of archaeologists and historians studying the Mound Builders, including evidence of trade, cities, and slavery.
- Explain that mounds were built as burial sites, temple platforms, and religious symbols.
- Summarize key theories on the disappearance of the Mound Builders, including disease and outside attack.

# PREPARE

Approximate lesson time is 60 minutes.

## Materials
For the Student

A History of US (Concise Edition), Volume A (Prehistory to 1800) by Joy Hakim

History Journal

The Mound Builders Assessment Sheet

## Keywords and Pronunciation
**Algonquian** (al-GAHN-kwee-uhn)

# LEARN
## Activity 1: Dig Those Mound Builders (Offline)
### Instructions
**Check Your Reading (Chapter 8, pages 38–41)**

- Go online and click Flash Cards to review Chapter 8.
- Complete the row for the Mound Builders on your Native American Groups sheet.

**Use What You Know**

There are several theories that try to explain the disappearance of the Mound Builders. You can read about them in Chapter 8. In your History Journal, write a short newspaper article with the headline: "Mound Builders Disappear!"

The first paragraph should be the *lead*. The lead is a short paragraph that answers most or all of the "five W's and how." The five W's are *who, what, where, when,* and *why*. The lead should also explain *how* things happened. Most newspaper articles begin with a lead.

There are two reasons to write a lead. One is to get the reader's attention. The other is to help readers learn the most important facts quickly. There are several ways to write a lead. Here are some of them:

- Write a sentence or two summing up the whole event.
- Start with a quotation from someone involved in the event.
- Describe the scene where the event took place.
- Ask an interesting question to catch the reader's attention.

The second paragraph should give more details about the topic. Include general information about the Mound Builders in this paragraph. Compare your paragraph with the sample in the Learning Coach Guide.

**Read On**

Between the Atlantic coast and the Mississippi River was a land carpeted with trees. The forests there teemed with life. Beaver, deer, raccoon, opossum, and bear made easy targets for the hunters who shared the woods. This is where the peoples of the eastern forests lived—the Algonquian tribes. We call them Woodland Indians. To the north of the Algonquians was a confederation of Indian nations, known as the Iroquois. Although they were enemies of the Algonquians, they believed in peace and brotherhood.

Read Chapter 9, pages 42–46. As you read, see if you can find the answers to these questions:

1. How were the Woodland Indians grouped?
2. Did the different groups get along?
3. What was the purpose of the Iroquois League?

Vocabulary

You'll see these words as you read. Write a brief definition for each as you come to it.

- Algonquian (al-GAHN-kwee-uhn)
- wigwam
- wampum
- confederacy

# ASSESS

## Lesson Assessment: The Mound Builders (*Offline*)

You will complete an offline assessment covering the main goals for the lesson. An adult will score the assessment and enter the results online.

Name _____  Date _____

# Lesson Assessment

1. Which area on the map did the Mound Builders live in?

   (A) 1

   (B) 2

   (C) 3

   (D) 4

   (E) 5

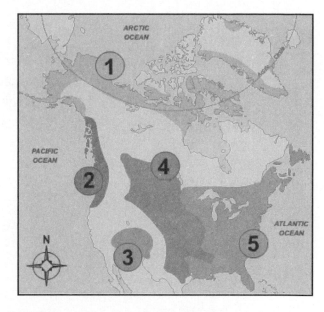

2. Give at least two reasons why the Mound Builders built their mounds.

   _____

   _____

   _____

3. What are two theories on why the cities of the Mound Builders, such as Cahokia, disappeared?

   _____

   _____

   _____

4. Describe at least two things that archaeologists and historians have learned about the Mound Builders.

   _____

   _____

   _____

# Student Guide
## Lesson 10: The Eastern Woodland Indians

The Algonquian peoples lived in the Eastern Woodlands. They lived in groups who spoke similar languages. They traded with one another. They hunted and gathered. They also practiced slash-and-burn farming. They had few enemies except for the Iroquois, whom they called the "terrible people."

## Lesson Objectives

- Locate the area where the Eastern Woodland Indians lived on a map.
- Identify and describe the shelter, food, customs, and beliefs of the Eastern Woodland Indians.
- Analyze drawings to gather information about some Eastern Woodland Indians.
- Explain that the purpose of the Iroquois League was to bring independent nations together for mutual defense and common concerns.
- Describe the role of women among the Iroquois as tribal leaders.

## PREPARE

Approximate lesson time is 60 minutes.

### Materials

For the Student

⌨ Document Analysis: Eastern Woodland Indians

A History of US (Concise Edition), Volume A (Prehistory to 1800) by Joy Hakim

History Journal

⌨ The Eastern Woodland Indians Assessment Sheet

## LEARN
### Activity 1: Indians of the Eastern Forests (Offline)
#### Instructions
#### Check Your Reading (Chapter 9, pages 42–46)

The Eastern Woodland Indians spoke an Algonquian language. They had a good life, but they had enemies to the north. Do you know who these enemies were?

- Go online and review Chapter 9 with the Flash Cards.
- Complete the row for the Eastern Woodland Indians in your Native American Groups table. Review Chapter 9 if you have trouble remembering the information you need.
- On a map of the United States, locate the area where the Eastern Woodland Indians lived.

**Use What You Know**

You analyzed photographs of life on the Northwest coast. Now do the same with drawings of Eastern Woodland Indians. Analyzing drawings is a lot like analyzing photographs. Just follow the directions on the Document Analysis sheet. Discuss your work with an adult.

---

# ASSESS

## Lesson Assessment: The Eastern Woodland Indians (*Offline*)

You will complete an offline assessment covering the main goals for the lesson. An adult will score the assessment and enter the results online.

Name _____    Date _____

# Document Analysis: Eastern Woodland Indians

You can learn a lot by studying, or analyzing, historical drawings. Drawing analysis, like photograph analysis, is a skill that historians use to learn about the past.

**Step 1: Observation**

On page 43 of Chapter 9 there are two pictures that were drawn by sixteenth-century artists who traveled to the New World. The one on the top shows Indians hunting deer. The one on the bottom shows Indians cultivating (farming) their land. We can learn a lot about the lives of the first Americans by studying historical drawings like these.

For each drawing, follow these steps.

1. Study the drawing. Form an impression of the whole drawing in your mind.
2. Now examine individual objects in the drawing.
3. Divide the drawing into four equal sections, or quadrants. Study each section. Look for details.
4. Complete the following chart. List people, objects, and activities you notice in the drawing.

| Drawing | People | Objects | Activities |
|---|---|---|---|
| 1. farming | | | |
| 4. hunting | | | |

**Step 2: Inference**

Based on your observations, list at least two things you might infer from each drawing. To infer is to draw a conclusion based on facts. For example, if you see a drawing of a person wearing lots of jewelry, you could infer that the person likes jewelry.

Drawing 1: farming

1. _____

2. _____

Drawing 2: hunting

1. _____

2. _____

**Step 3: Questions**

What questions come to mind when you study these drawings? Where could you find the answers to these questions? Select one drawing to ask these questions about.

Drawing: _____

1. What questions come to mind when you study this drawing? _____

_____

_____

2. Where could you find the answers to those questions? _____

_____

_____

Name _____ Date _____

## Lesson Assessment

1. Which area on the map did the Eastern Woodland Indians live in?

   Ⓐ 1

   Ⓑ 2

   Ⓒ 3

   Ⓓ 4

   Ⓔ 5

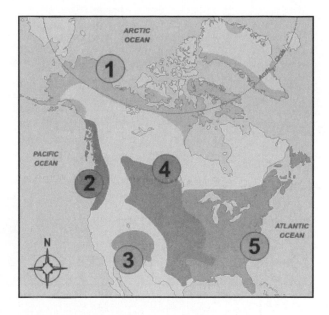

2. Describe the type of shelter that Eastern Woodland Indians lived in.

   _____

   _____

3. Describe the work done by the men and women of a typical Eastern Woodland Indian village.

   _____

   _____

   _____

# *Student Guide*
## Lesson 11: Unit Review

You've completed Unit 1, The Earliest Americans. It's time to review what you've learned. You'll take the Unit Assessment in the next lesson.

### Lesson Objectives
- Review major characteristics of Native American groups.
- Compare and contrast Native American groups in terms of location, food, clothing, shelter, economic activity, and government.

---

# PREPARE

Approximate lesson time is 60 minutes.

## Materials
For the Student

A History of US (Concise Edition), Volume A (Prehistory to 1800) by Joy Hakim

History Journal

---

# LEARN
## Activity 1: A Look Back *(Offline)*
### Instructions
### Online Review

Review the Big Picture and the Flash Cards to get started.

### History Journal Review

Continue reviewing by going through your History Journal.

- Look at the sheets you completed for this unit.
- Review your vocabulary words.
- Read over the writing assignments you completed.

Take your time. Your History Journal is a great resource for a unit review!

---

# Student Guide
## Lesson 12: Unit Assessment

You've finished this unit! Now take the Unit Assessment.

## Lesson Objectives

- Recognize the role of an archaeologist.
- Locate the Bering Sea and land bridge on a map or globe.
- Trace the migration route of the earliest Americans.
- Locate the regions where Inuit live on a map.
- Describe and categorize Inuit shelter, food, customs, and beliefs.
- Locate on a map the area where the cliff dwellers lived.
- Describe Anasazi shelter, food, customs, and beliefs.
- Locate the area where the Northwest Indians lived on a map.
- Describe Northwest Indian shelter, food, beliefs, and customs, including totem poles.
- Identify and describe Plains Indians shelter, food, customs, beliefs, and nomadic way of life.
- Describe the findings of archaeologists and historians studying the Mound Builders, including evidence of trade, cities, and slavery.
- Locate the area where the Eastern Woodland Indians lived on a map.
- Identify and describe the shelter, food, customs, and beliefs of the Eastern Woodland Indians.
- Define *sachem* and *wampum*.
- Explain that the purpose of the Iroquois League was to bring independent nations together for mutual defense and common concerns.
- Use maps and globes to locate places.
- Identify Pueblo peoples as the Anasazi's modern descendants.
- Describe three changes that occurred as a result of the Spanish introduction of the horse to North America.
- Explain that the Plains Indians depended on the buffalo for food, clothing, shelter, and tools.

---

# PREPARE

Approximate lesson time is 60 minutes.

## Materials

For the Student

place mat map

📖 The Earliest Americans Assessment Sheet

# ASSESS

## Unit Assessment: The Earliest Americans (*Offline*)

Complete the offline Unit Assessment. Your Learning Coach will score it and enter the results online.

Name _____ Date _____

# Unit Assessment

Use your place mat map of the United States to answer the following question.

**1.** If you were to travel from Virginia to Missouri, in what direction would you be going? ____

Answer questions 2 through 4 by marking the following map.

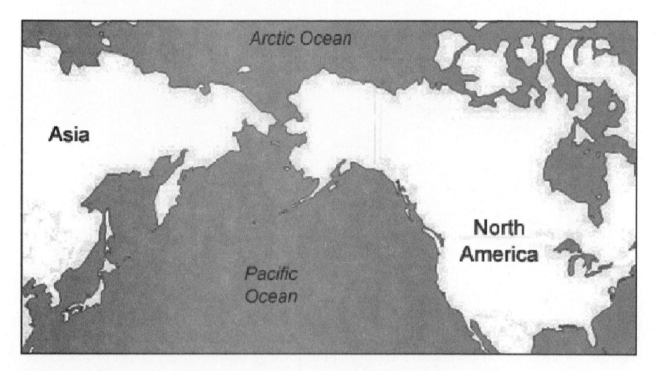

**2.** Label the Bering Strait on the map.

**3.** The first Americans crossed over a land bridge. Draw a rectangle around the area where this land bridge existed.

**4.** Draw an arrow to show the migration route of the first Americans.

**5.** Fill in the bubble in front of the true statement.

Ⓐ Climate changes with latitude. The closer to the equator, the warmer it is.

Ⓑ Climate changes with latitude. The closer to the equator, the colder it is.

Ⓒ Climate is not affected by latitude.

Ⓓ Climate changes with latitude. The higher the degree of latitude, the warmer it is.

**6.** On the map below, write the letter of each of the following Native American cultural groups in the appropriate space.

    **A.** Eastern Woodland

    **B.** Inuit

    **C.** Anasazi

    **D.** Northwest

    **E.** Plains

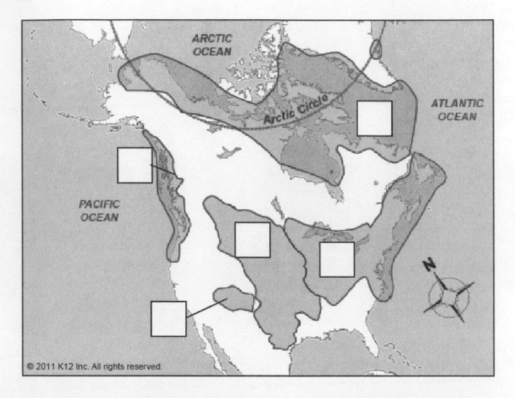

© 2011 K12 Inc. All rights reserved.

*(6 points)*

**7.** Match each Native American group on the left with the description on the right. Write the letter of the description on the line in front of the group's name.

_____ Inuit

_____ Indians of the Northwest

_____ Anasazi

_____ Plains Indians

_____ Mound Builders

_____ Eastern Woodland Indians

**A.** Built large cities; traded far and wide

**B.** Farmed the deset; decendents built pueblos

**C.** Lived in igloos; used blubber for many things

**D.** Valued wealth and prestige; hunted whales

**E.** Depended on the buffalo; horses changed their lives

**F.** Lived in wigwams and longhouses; women farmed

**G.** Migrated from South America; built great stone temples

**8.** Fill in the bubble in front of the statement that is true about Native Americans.

Ⓐ They all lived in tepees and wigwams and hunted on horseback.

Ⓑ They all fought wars and used their captured enemies as slaves.

Ⓒ They all shared a common respect for nature and the land.

Ⓓ They all developed societies that mysteriously disappeared.

*(7 points)*

**9.** Match each word on the left with its definition on the right. Write the letter of the definition on the line in front of the word.

| | |
|---|---|
| _____ migration | **A.** A region with sparse vegetation that receives little rain |
| _____ climate zone | **B.** A scientist who studies materials from the past |
| _____ desert | **C.** A confederacy of Eastern Woodland Indian nations |
| _____ archaeologist | **D.** An area with a distinct temperature and precipitation range |
| _____ culture region | **E.** An Indian group that lived in the Pacific Northwest |
| | **F.** A group of Indians who shared similar languages |
| _____ Algonquian language group | **G.** An area where people share similar ways of life |
| _____ Iroquois League | **H.** Movement from one place to another |

*(3 points)*

**10.** Describe the ways in which the Plains Indians used the buffalo. Include at least three uses. (Write your answer in complete sentences.)

_____

_____

_____

_____

**(7 points)**

**11.** Match each word on the left with its definition on the right. Write the letter of the definition on the line in front of the word.

_____ pueblo

_____ nomad

_____ wampum

_____ matrilineal

_____ adobe

_____ plain

_____ totem pole

**A.** A wide area of flat or rolling land with few trees

**B.** A village built by the descendants of the Anasazi

**C.** A person who moves from place to place within a well-defined territory

**D.** A domed shelter made of ice

**E.** Tiny shell beads strung on cords and woven into designs to tell a story

**F.** Tall pole on which animal and human figures are carved

**G.** Describes a society that traces descent through the mother

**H.** Sun-dried clay mud used to make houses in the Southwest

**(2 points)**

**12.** Describe at least two ways that the horse changed the way the Plains Indians lived. (Write your answer in complete sentences.)

_____

_____

_____

_____

# Student Guide
## Lesson 1: Navigating Uncharted Waters

The 16th century was a time of tremendous change and excitement in much of Europe. A growing thirst for knowledge, power, and wealth led to remarkable voyages of exploration. Those voyages, in turn, led to unimaginable discoveries for Europeans and the greatest exchange of plant and animal life in history. The period begins before the tomato in Italy, the potato in Ireland, or the horse on the Great Plains. It ends with huge population growth in Europe, decimation of populations in the Americas, and the eventual forced migration of 12 million Africans.

Most historians believe the Vikings were the first Europeans to sail to North America. How far they explored is still a mystery. Four centuries later, other Europeans set sail across oceans. New learning and technology had opened the world to Europeans. The printing press made books and maps affordable, so ideas spread. An improved compass helped ships sail farther from home. Many Europeans wanted to trade with the rich lands of Asia. They wanted to find a route that would let them sail there.

### Lesson Objectives

- Identify the Vikings as the first Europeans to make settlements in North America.
- Use maps to plot longitude, latitude, and direction.

# PREPARE

Approximate lesson time is 60 minutes.

### Materials

For the Student

A History of US (Concise Edition), Volume A (Prehistory to 1800) by Joy Hakim

map, world

# LEARN
## Activity 1: The Vikings (Offline)
### Instructions
### Read

Read Chapter 10, pages 47–49.

Vocabulary

You'll see these terms as you read. Write a brief definition for each term as you come to it:

- Scandinavia
- anthropology

## Use What You Know

Use the place mat map of the world to trace routes and write navigation log entries in your History Journal.

Both Viking, and later European, explorers could tell how far north or south they had traveled by sighting known stars to identify their position. They had to guess how far they had traveled east or west, however. A compass would tell them which direction they were traveling, but it wouldn't tell them how far they had gone.

Pretend that you're a Viking on a journey from Norway to North America. Write at least four navigation log entries in your History Journal. Include the following:

1. The day (guess how long it would take to get to each point)
2. The land you sighted (as it is labeled on the world map)
3. The direction you traveled
4. Your approximate position in degrees of latitude.

Here is your first entry as an example. (You've reached the United Kingdom.)

Day 2
First land sighted since we left home. It is the United Kingdom.
Traveled southwest.
Position is 59° N.

## Read On

On the place mat map of the world, point to Spain, Cuba, and China. Columbus wanted to sail west from Spain to China. You see what got in his way.

Read about Christopher Columbus and how he believed that the world was round. You will learn about his search for support for his plans, his first voyage, and what he discovered.

- Read Chapter 11, pages 50–55, and Chapter 12, pages 56–59.
- Be prepared to evaluate Columbus on the success of his efforts.

## Vocabulary

You'll see these words as you read. Write a brief definition for each in your History Journal as you come to it.

- hemisphere
- parallel
- meridian
- astrolabe (AS-truh-layb)
- Taino (TIY-noh)

# Student Guide
## Lesson 2: Discovering New Lands

As a child, Christopher Columbus dreamed of sailing to China. As an old man, he died thinking he had done just that. He knew a lot about geography, but missed some clues that would have prevented a big mistake. He believed the world was round, but he misjudged how big it was. He set sail on an exciting and frightening journey across the Atlantic Ocean to find China. Instead, on October 12, 1492, Columbus landed in America and met the native peoples who lived there.

## Lesson Objectives

- Identify Columbus as the first explorer to attempt to reach East Asia by sailing west from Europe.
- Recognize Columbus's errors in understanding the distance around the Earth and in thinking he had reached Asia.
- Define primary source and analyze a primary source to gain information.
- Explain the significance of new knowledge and inventions in fifteenth-century Europe, including Gutenberg's press and the compass.
- Explain the reasons for European desire to go to Asia, including an interest in learning and the desire for power, wealth, and goods.
- Identify the Vikings as the first Europeans to make settlements in North America.

# PREPARE

Approximate lesson time is 60 minutes.

## Materials

For the Student

📖 Document Analysis: Columbus's Letter

A History of US (Concise Edition), Volume A (Prehistory to 1800) by Joy Hakim

Understanding Geography: Map Skills and Our World (Level 5)

map, world

# LEARN
## Activity 1: Columbus "Discovers" America—By Mistake *(Offline)*
### Instructions
Check Your Reading (Chapter 11, pages 50–55, and Chapter 12, pages 56–59)

Answer the following questions in your History Journal. Use a world map to help you answer questions 1 and 2.

1.  Find the Tropic of Cancer on your globe. This line of latitude is at 23½° N. What is another name for lines of latitude?
2.  Columbus's plan was to follow the parallel of the Tropic of Cancer to China. Why would he choose to navigate that route? How did the navigational instruments he had influence that decision?
3.  Why did Columbus believe he had reached Asia when he had actually sailed less than halfway there?
4.  How did the improved compass help Europeans explore farther from their home ports?
5.  Columbus and other European explorers read about Marco Polo's adventures in China. They studied maps and read about new scientific discoveries. That new knowledge helped promote European exploration. What invention, made in 1456, allowed that knowledge and information to spread quickly?

## Document Analysis

Primary sources are one of the things historians use to learn about the past. Primary sources are documents made by people who actually saw or participated in an event and recorded that event soon afterward. They can be drawings, paintings, photographs, or written documents such as letters, reports, diaries, or newspaper articles.

Complete the Document Analysis: Columbus's Letter sheet.

## Map Scales

Learn how to calculate distances on maps.

- Read Activity 4, "Map Scales" (pages 16–19), in *Understanding Geography*.
- Answer questions 1–11 in your History Journal.
- If you have time, you may want to answer the Skill Builder Questions on page 19.
- After you have finished you should compare your answers with the ones in the Learning Coach Guide.

## Read On

Columbus made several more journeys to the Americas. In doing so, he brought many things with him from Europe and took many things back to Europe from the Americas. The world has never been the same since.

- Read Chapter 13, pages 60–65.
- Prepare to discuss what happened as a result of the Columbian Exchange.

## Beyond the Lesson

Go online to learn more about Christopher Columbus.

# ASSESS
## Lesson Assessment: Discovering New Lands (*Online*)

# LEARN
## Activity 2. Optional: More on Columbus (*Online*)

Name _____  Date _____

## Document Analysis: Columbus's Letter

You can learn a lot by studying, or analyzing, documents such as letters. Document analysis is a skill that historians use to learn about the past. Primary source documents are created by people who actually saw or participated in an event and recorded that event soon afterward. When considering the value of a primary source document, these are some of the things it is important to know:

- What type of document it is
- The name and position (title) of the person who wrote it
- When it was written
- Whom it was written for

Answer the following questions based on the primary source "From Columbus's Pen" in Chapter 12.

1. What type of document is this? _____

2. Is this a primary source document? _____

3. When was it written? _____

4. Who was the author? _____

5. What was the author's position or title? _____

6. For whom was the document written? _____

7. List three things the author said that you think are important.

   _____

   _____

   _____

8. Why do you think this document was written? _____

   _____

   _____

9. What evidence in the document helps you know why it was written? Quote from the document. _____

_____

_____

_____

10. List two things the document tells you about life in the Americas at the time that it was written. _____

_____

_____

_____

11. Write a question to the author that the document leaves unanswered.

_____

_____

_____

# Student Guide
## Lesson 3: Columbus Journeys On

Columbus didn't find gold or a route to China on his second voyage. And he still didn't realize he was not in Asia. Instead he brought the first of a flood of Europeans and Africans to the Americas. These people brought plants, animals, and diseases that were new to the Western Hemisphere. Then they introduced plants, animals, and diseases of the Americas to Europe and Africa. The world was changed forever.

### Lesson Objectives
- Use maps to gain information on the Columbian Exchange.
- Recognize that plants, animals and diseases were exchanged among continents as a result of European exploration.
- Explain the reason for the introduction of African slavery into the Americas as a way to fill the need for field workers.
- List at least four plants, three animals, and one disease that were part of the Columbian Exchange.
- Demonstrate knowledge gained in previous lessons.
- Define *hemisphere, parallel*, and *meridian*.
- Identify Columbus as the first explorer to attempt to reach East Asia by sailing west from Europe.
- Recognize Columbus's errors in understanding the distance around the Earth and in thinking he had reached Asia.
- Define primary source and analyze a primary source to gain information.

# PREPARE

Approximate lesson time is 60 minutes.

### Materials
For the Student

A History of US (Concise Edition), Volume A (Prehistory to 1800) by Joy Hakim

History Journal

🖳 Columbus Journeys On Assessment Sheet

# LEARN
## Activity 1: When Two Worlds Collide (Online)
### Instructions
Check Your Reading (Chapter 13, pages 60–65)

Review Chapter 13 by answering the following questions in your History Journal:

1. What was exchanged among continents as a result of European exploration of North and South America?
2. Why were black people from Africa brought to the Caribbean Islands as slaves?

Ask an adult to check your answers.

## Use What You Know

Life existed for thousands of years with little contact between the Eastern Hemisphere and the Western Hemisphere. When Columbus bridged those two worlds, the exchange between the Old World and the New World began. Some parts of that exchange happened right away, while others are still going on.
Go back online to read Worlds of Change—The Columbian Exchange to learn more about this exchange. Be prepared to identify at least four plants, three animals, and one disease that were part of the Columbian Exchange.

When you've finished, write the answers to the following questions in complete sentences in your History Journal. Check your answers with an adult.

1. Identify four plants, three animals, and one disease that were a part of the Columbian Exchange.
2. In North and South America, most people are of European or African descent. Can you explain why so few Native Americans exist in their own land?
3. Explain how and why millions of African slaves were brought to the New World.
4. In the sixteenth and seventeenth centuries, huge population shifts occurred in the Americas that related to four continents—two in the Eastern Hemisphere and two in the Western Hemisphere. Identify the continents and describe the population shifts.
5. One Native American group in North America was particularly changed by the introduction of an animal to the New World. Which Indian group was changed by what animal? How was it changed?
6. Two large animals that were introduced to the New World changed whole societies and helped create cultures and industries in both North and South America. What were these animals? What culture did they help create? What two industries did one of those animals help create?

## Look Back

Advances in technology, a European desire to sail to Asia, and a visionary named Columbus came together to start a whole new chapter in the history of the world.

Review the following to prepare for an assessment:

- Chapters 10–13 in *A History of US (Concise Edition),* Volume A (Prehistory to 1800)
- History Journal

Online, review:

- Worlds of Change—The Columbian Exchange
- Columbus Flash Cards

If you have difficulty with any part of the material, review it with an adult.

**Read On**

Aztec civilization was sophisticated, with a magnificent capital city and the largest army in the world. What happened when the Aztecs met the Spaniards? Where did all that magnificence and power go?

- Read Chapter 15, pages 71–75.
- Prepare to discuss what happened to the Aztecs after they met the Spaniards.

Vocabulary

You'll see these terms as you read. Write a brief definition for each term in your History Journal.

- artisans
- Mesoamerica

**Optional: Beyond the Lesson**

Read Chapter 14, pages 66–70, to learn about some of the explorers that sailed into uncharted waters in the early sixteenth century.

---

# ASSESS
## Mid-Unit Assessment: Columbus Journeys On (*Offline*)

You will complete an offline assessment covering the main goals for Lessons 1, 2, and 3. An adult will score the assessment and enter the results online.

---

# LEARN
## Activity 2. Optional: Finding the Pacific and Sailing Around the World (*Online*)

Name _____ Date _____

# Mid-Unit Assessment

1. Match each word on the left with its definition on the right. Write the letter of the definition on the line in front of the word.

| | |
|---|---|
| _____ meridian | **A.** The movement of plants, animals, diseases, and people between the Eastern Hemisphere and the Western Hemisphere after 1492 |
| _____ primary source | **B.** Another term for a line of latitude |
| | **C.** Another term for a line of longitude |
| _____ hemisphere | **D.** The Caribbean island where Columbus made his base for a trading post |
| _____ Columbian Exchange | **E.** The name of Columbus's flagship |
| | **F.** One half of the earth—divided, for example, at the equator |
| _____ parallel | |
| | **G.** A document created by people who saw or participated in an event and recorded that event soon afterward |
| _____ Hispaniola | |

2. Who was the first explorer to attempt to reach East Asia by sailing west from Europe?

(A) Amerigo Vespucci

(B) Marco Polo

(C) Christopher Columbus

(D) Leif Eriksson

3. What mistake did Columbus make that led him to believe he could make it to Asia by sailing west?

(A) He miscalculated the size of the earth by more than half.

(B) He gave in to his sailors when they threatened mutiny.

(C) He got Spanish financial and political backing.

4. Which of the following statements is true about relations between Columbus and the Native Americans?

(A) They enjoyed a long and prosperous trading relationship.

(B) At first Columbus and the Native Americans fought, but then they made peace.

(C) Good relations turned bad when Columbus realized the Native Americans had little to offer him.

(D) Columbus attacked every Native American he met.

5. African slavery was introduced to the Americas because _____.

(A) a potato famine in Africa forced millions of starving Africans into slavery

(B) the Spanish conquered Africa and took millions of Africans as slaves

(C) the Spanish needed a large army to defeat the Native Americans

(D) slaves were needed to work the sugar plantations

6. List four plants, three animals, and one disease that were introduced to lands where they had never existed before 1492.

| Plants | Animals | Diseases |
|--------|---------|----------|
| _____ | _____ | _____ |
| _____ | _____ | |
| _____ | _____ | |
| _____ | | |

# Student Guide
## Lesson 4: The Spanish Conquest

Two worlds came together when the Spaniard Hernando Cortés met the Aztec ruler Moctezuma. The battle fought in Tenochtitlán, the Aztec capital, decided the fate of this mighty Mesoamerican civilization.

### Lesson Objectives
- Locate the Aztec Empire on a map.
- Identify Moctezuma as the leader of the Aztecs and Cortés as their Spanish conqueror.
- Describe the Aztec Empire as a complex civilization.
- Identify Mesoamerica and three Mesoamerican civilizations before the Spanish conquest.

---

# PREPARE

Approximate lesson time is 60 minutes.

### Materials
For the Student

 💻 European Explorers

 💻 Map of European Exploration

 💻 Senor Hernando Cortes

 A History of US (Concise Edition), Volume A (Prehistory to 1800) by Joy Hakim

 History Journal

---

# LEARN
## Activity 1: New Spain (Offline)
### Instructions
Check Your Reading (Chapter 15, pages 71–75)

Review Chapter 15 by looking at a map and completing an activity sheet.

- On the map of European Exploration, find the route Cortés took from Cuba to Tenochtitlán. Add his route to the European Explorers sheet using a colored pencil or marker. Then add that color to the legend. Keep the sheet in your History Journal. You will need it for later lessons.
- Complete the Señor Hernando Cortés sheet. Have an adult check your answers.

A Very Short History of Mesoamerica

Answer the following questions in your History Journal. Have an adult check your work.

1. What does *Mesoamerica* mean?
2. Which was the first Mesoamerican civilization to develop? What agricultural contribution did that group make to Mesoamerican civilization?
3. What kind of system of writing did the Maya develop?
4. What were some of the accomplishments of the Mayan civilization?
5. Which Mesoamericans were warriors who built monumental pyramids?

## Read On

Ponce de León, the "brave lion," discovered Florida while searching for the Fountain of Youth. Francisco Pizarro defeated the large and powerful Inca Empire with just 180 men. Francisco Vasquez de Coronado searched for cities of gold. Read about these explorers and learn why the Spanish were so eager to explore the New World.

- Read Chapter 16, pages 76–80, and Chapter 17, pages 81–84.
- Be prepared to explain why people in Europe accepted the brutal destruction of Native American civilizations.

## Optional: Beyond the Lesson

Visit a website to read an article about the discovery of an ancient Mesoamerican ball court.

# Activity 2. Optional: The Spanish Conquest *(Online)*

# European Exploration

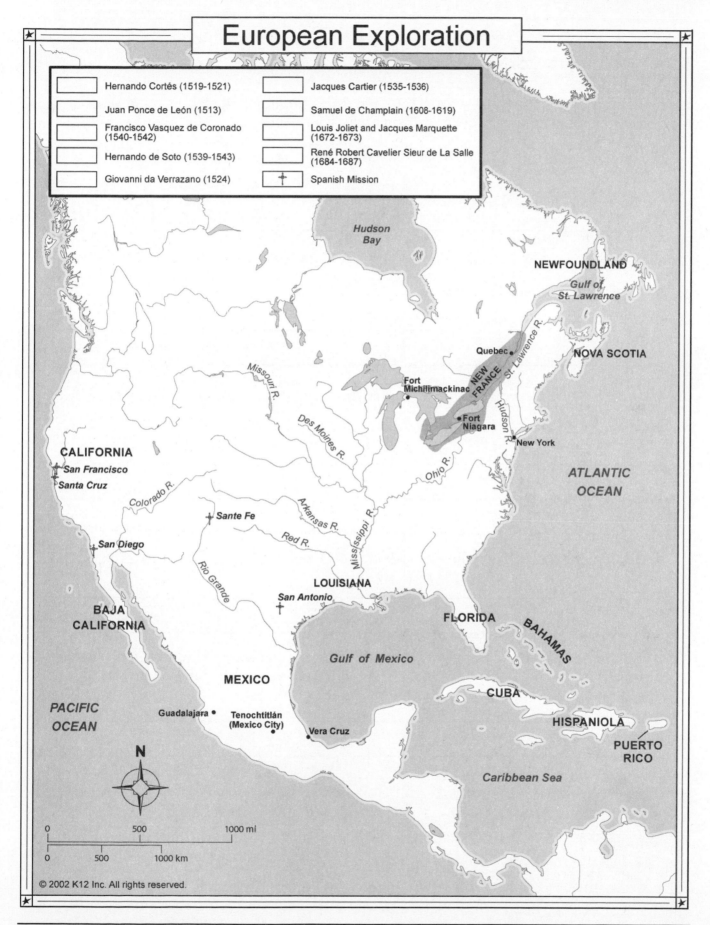

| | Hernando Cortés (1519-1521) | | Jacques Cartier (1535-1536) |
| --- | --- | --- | --- |
| | Juan Ponce de León (1513) | | Samuel de Champlain (1608-1619) |
| | Francisco Vasquez de Coronado (1540-1542) | | Louis Joliet and Jacques Marquette (1672-1673) |
| | Hernando de Soto (1539-1543) | | René Robert Cavelier Sieur de La Salle (1684-1687) |
| | Giovanni da Verrazano (1524) | ✝ | Spanish Mission |

Hudson Bay

NEWFOUNDLAND

Gulf of St. Lawrence

NOVA SCOTIA

Quebec

NEW FRANCE

St. Lawrence R.

Missouri R.

Fort Michilimackinac

Des Moines R.

Fort Niagara

Hudson R.

New York

CALIFORNIA

San Francisco

Santa Cruz

Ohio R.

ATLANTIC OCEAN

Colorado R.

Sante Fe

Arkansas R.

San Diego

Red R.

Mississippi R.

Rio Grande

LOUISIANA

San Antonio

BAJA CALIFORNIA

FLORIDA

BAHAMAS

Gulf of Mexico

MEXICO

CUBA

PACIFIC OCEAN

Guadalajara

Tenochtitlán (Mexico City)

Vera Cruz

HISPANIOLA

PUERTO RICO

Caribbean Sea

N

0        500        1000 mi

0    500    1000 km

Name _____  Date _____

## Señor Hernando Cortés

Señor Hernando Cortés, you have just returned from your trip to the lands in the West. Would you mind answering a few questions about your experiences?

1. Would you describe for us what impressed you most about Tenochtitlán?

   _____

   _____

2. We understand that you were horrified by some Aztec customs. Would you describe the practices that bothered you most? _____

   _____

   _____

3. Your men claim that you burned and sank your own ships! Is this true, and if so, why on earth would you do such a thing? _____

   _____

   _____

4. The Aztecs ruled over a great empire and were much feared by their enemies. How did you conquer such a mighty enemy with only 400 men? _____

   _____

   _____

5. It is rumored that your campaign was greatly helped by a woman named Doña Marina. Who was she and what, if anything, did she do to aid you against the enemy?

   _____

   _____

**Thinking Cap Question!** Tenochtitlán amazed Cortés and his men. Draw a picture or write a story that shows how Tenochtitlán was different from their home, Madrid, and from other European cities.

Adapted from *A History of US*

# Student Guide
## Lesson 5: Ponce de León and Coronado

Spanish conquistadors dreamed of finding another rich empire to conquer. They drove deeper into the Americas. Spain's thirst for gold did not end with the brutal conquest of the Incas. It was the reason for Coronado's 7,000-mile journey in search of the fabled city of Cíbola.

### Lesson Objectives
- Identify Ponce de León as a Spanish explorer of Florida.
- Locate Puerto Rico, Florida, and Cuba on a map.
- Identify Francisco Vasquez de Coronado as a Spanish explorer of the southwestern United States and trace his route on a map.

---

# PREPARE

Approximate lesson time is 60 minutes.

### Materials
> For the Student
>> 🖥 Picture Puzzles
>>
>> A History of US (Concise Edition), Volume A (Prehistory to 1800) by Joy Hakim
>>
>> History Journal

---

# LEARN
## Activity 1: Spain Seeks Riches in the New World *(Offline)*
### Instructions
**Check Your Reading (Chapter 16, pages 76–80, and Chapter 17, pages 81–84)**

- Add the routes of Ponce de León and Francisco Vasquez de Coronado to the European Explorers sheet from the Spanish Conquest lesson. (Refer to the map of European Exploration from the same lesson.) Also label Florida, Cuba, and Puerto Rico. Keep these sheets in your History Journal.
- Complete the Picture Puzzles sheet. Discuss your answers with an adult.

**Use What You Know**

During their journeys, many explorers kept diaries or journals in which they recorded their observations, thoughts, and feelings. Some explorers also drew maps showing where they went.

Imagine you are traveling with Coronado as he leads his expedition to find Cíbola. In your History Journal, write a journal entry about your adventure.

---

The journal entry should:

- Describe the makeup of the expedition (who went, how they traveled, what they ate, what they brought, etc.).
- Describe at least one encounter with Indians.
- Describe the findings of one exploring party that Coronado sent out.
- Express your opinion as to whether the expedition was a success or not and why.
- Include a map showing the expedition's route.

**Read On**

Ponce de León and Coronado weren't the last conquistadors to come to America. Hernando de Soto came to explore Florida and ended up discovering the Mississippi River. The dream of finding Cíbola hadn't died, either. Juan de Oñate would set out to find the golden city. Of course we know he didn't find it. But he would start a Spanish colony in New Mexico—Santa Fe.

- Read Chapter 18, pages 85–88, and Chapter 19, pages 89–92.
- Prepare to trace Hernando de Soto's route of exploration across the southeastern United States.

Name _____     Date _____

## Picture Puzzles

Study the pictures and review Chapters 16 and 17 to answer these questions.

1. The place is Peru. Who is fighting? Who won?
   What conquistador was in charge?

   _____

   _____

   _____

   _____

   _____

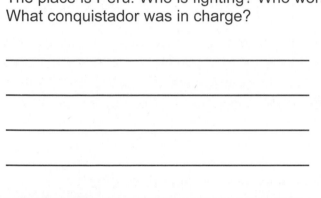

2. The place is Cuzco. Why are the people
   gathering all of their gold?

   _____

   _____

   _____

   _____

3. Who made this silver alpaca? What happened to most of their

   artwork? _____

   _____

4. What happened to about three-quarters of all Native Americans
   after Europeans arrived in the Americas?

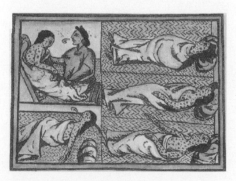

   _____

   _____

   **Thinking Cap Question!** In the sixteenth century,
   Europeans were looking for gold and not much else.
   What if they had valued the arts and culture of the people
   they met? Explain how you think history might have been
   different.

Adapted from *A History of US*

# Student Guide
## Lesson 6: More Conquistadors

Conquistadors continued to explore North America. Cabrillo and de Soto explored California and the southeastern United States. They failed to find gold. Finally, one Spaniard did what no other had done. Juan de Oñate established a Spanish colony north of New Spain—Santa Fe.

### Lesson Objectives
- Identify Hernando de Soto as a Spanish explorer of the southeastern United States and trace on a map his route of exploration.
- Describe the behavior of the conquistadors toward the Native Americans.
- Identify one city in the United States that started as a Spanish mission.
- Locate the Aztec Empire on a map.
- Identify Moctezuma as the leader of the Aztecs and Cortés as their Spanish conqueror.
- Describe the Aztec Empire as a complex civilization.
- Identify Mesoamerica and three Mesoamerican civilizations before the Spanish conquest.
- Identify Ponce de León as a Spanish explorer of Florida.
- Locate Puerto Rico, Florida, and Cuba on a map.
- Identify Francisco Vasquez de Coronado as a Spanish explorer of the southwestern United States and trace his route on a map.

# PREPARE

Approximate lesson time is 60 minutes.

### Materials
For the Student
    A History of US (Concise Edition), Volume A (Prehistory to 1800) by Joy Hakim
    map, U.S.
    History Journal
    🖳 European Exploration Assessment Sheet

# LEARN
## Activity 1: Giving Way to Priests and Settlers (Offline)
### Instructions
Check Your Reading (Chapter 18, pages 85–88, and Chapter 19, pages 89–92)

Add Hernando de Soto's route to the European Explorers sheet in your History Journal. Then update the legend.

Review Chapters 18 and 19 by answering these questions:

1. How did De Soto treat Native Americans he encountered during his westward trek out of Florida?
2. Suppose De Soto and Coronado had met. What would they have learned from each other?
3. What was the significance of the expedition led by Juan de Oñate?
4. How did the Spanish arrival in the American Southwest affect Native Americans living in the area?
5. How would you describe the behavior of the conquistadors toward Native Americans?
6. Name two U.S. cities that started as Spanish missions.

**Use What You Know**

Questions for Conquistadors

Write one or more questions in your History Journal that you would like to ask the conquistadors about their behavior toward Native Americans. Then decide whether you would have wanted to be a conquistador if you had lived at that time. Explain your decision.

Use the Flash Cards to review for the Mid-Unit Assessment.

**Read On**

Why were the French interested in a pirate base in Florida? And what were they up to in Canada?
Read Chapter 20, pages 93–98, and Chapter 21, pages 99–105.

**Beyond the Lesson**

Visit PBS online to further explore the Spanish conquest.

---

# ASSESS
## Mid-Unit Assessment: European Exploration (*Offline*)
You will complete an offline Mid-Unit Assessment covering Lessons 4, 5, and 6. An adult will score the assessment and enter the results online.

---

# LEARN
## Activity 2. Optional: More Conquistadors (*Online*)

---

Name _____ Date _____

# Mid-Unit Assessment

1. Match each person on the left with the description of the person on the right. Write the letter of the description on the line in front of the person.

_____ Moctezuma

_____ Cortés

_____ Ponce de León

_____ Coronado

_____ De Soto

A. Spanish conquistador who led a well-planned expedition to find Cíbola; traveled 7,000 miles across much of the southwestern United States

B. Aztec leader who ruled over a mighty empire in central Mexico; couldn't decide if invading Spaniards were gods or men

C. Conquistador who explored Florida and the southeastern United States; encouraged his men to torture, burn, and kill Indians; discovered the Mississippi River

D. Led the Spanish conquest of Mexico; with Indian allies, captured Tenochtitlán and conquered the Aztecs

E. "Brave lion" who found gold on the island of Puerto Rico; searched for a magical fountain in Florida; died from an Indian's poisoned arrow

F. Spanish explorer who discovered gold in Cíbola and then traveled from Kansas to California to establish missions along the Pacific coast

2. Which of the following best describes the Aztec Empire before it was conquered?

Ⓐ a small, complex civilization

Ⓑ a small, primitive civilization

Ⓒ a large, complex civilization

Ⓓ a large, primitive civilization

**3.** What does Mesoamerica mean?

Ⓐ Native America

Ⓑ Middle America

Ⓒ American civilizations

Ⓓ Mexican cultures

**4.** Which of the following was not a pre-Aztec Mesoamerican civilization?

Ⓐ the Inuit

Ⓑ the Olmecs

Ⓒ the Toltecs

Ⓓ the Maya

Use the following map to answer questions 5–10.

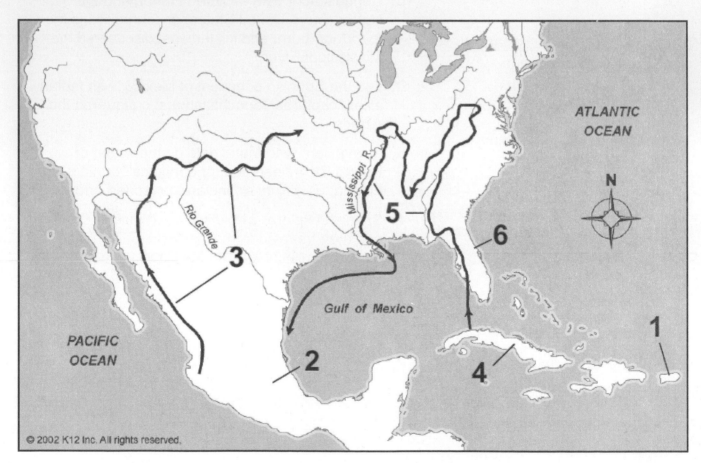

5. Which number correctly labels Coronado's route of exploration?

Ⓐ 1

Ⓑ 2

Ⓒ 3

Ⓓ 4

Ⓔ 5

Ⓕ 6

6. Which number correctly labels Hernando de Soto's route of exploration?

Ⓐ 1

Ⓑ 2

Ⓒ 3

Ⓓ 4

Ⓔ 5

Ⓕ 6

7. Which number correctly labels Puerto Rico?

Ⓐ 1

Ⓑ 2

Ⓒ 3

Ⓓ 4

Ⓔ 5

Ⓕ 6

8. Which number correctly labels Florida?

Ⓐ 1

Ⓑ 2

Ⓒ 3

Ⓓ 4

Ⓔ 5

Ⓕ 6

**9.** Which number correctly labels Cuba?

(A) 1

(B) 2

(C) 3

(D) 4

(E) 5

(F) 6

**10.** Which number correctly identifies the location of the Aztec Empire?

(A) 1

(B) 2

(C) 3

(D) 4

(E) 5

(F) 6

**11.** Describe at least two behaviors of the conquistadors toward the Native Americans they encountered.

_____

_____

_____

_____

**12.** Which of these U.S. cities began as a Spanish mission?

(A) Miami

(B) Santa Fe

(C) Houston

(D) Phoenix

# Student Guide
## Lesson 7: The French Explore America

The French came to the Americas as explorers and pirates. Some came to build settlements and escape religious persecution. They pushed north into Canada. Finally, their explorations took them down the Mississippi River to the doorstep of New Spain. We can still see their footsteps on maps today.

### Lesson Objectives

- Describe the economic and religious motives for French exploration and colonization in North America.
- Identify the area of North America claimed by the French and the routes of major explorers.
- Locate on a map the Mississippi River, Great Lakes, St. Lawrence River, Gulf of Mexico, and the Atlantic and Pacific Oceans.
- Identify major types of bodies of water.

# PREPARE

Approximate lesson time is 60 minutes.

## Materials

For the Student

A History of US (Concise Edition), Volume A (Prehistory to 1800) by Joy Hakim

Understanding Geography: Map Skills and Our World (Level 5)

History Journal

# LEARN
## Activity 1: Pirates, Adventurers, and New France (Offline)
### Instructions
**Check Your Reading (Chapter 20, pages 93–98, and Chapter 21, pages 99–105)**

Add the following explorers to the European Explorers sheet in your History Journal. (Refer to the map of European Exploration.)

- Giovanni da Verrazano
- Samuel de Champlain
- Louis Joliet and Jacques Marquette
- René Robert Cavelier Sieur de La Salle
- Jacques Cartier

Label *New France* and the *Mississippi River.*

Use the following words to describe the location of the Northwest Passage: Cathay, Eastern Ocean, river passage, Europe, North America. Have an adult check your description.

**Bodies of Water**

In the late 1600s, Europeans crossed the ocean and began exploring the New World and making claims to the lands they "discovered." Maps can help you understand historical events such as these. Maps can also give you clues about the history of a place.

- Read Activity 6, "Bodies of Water," pages 24–27, *Understanding Geography*.
- Answer Questions 1–22 in your History Journal.
- If you have time, you may want to answer the Skill Builder Questions on page 27.
- After you have finished, compare your answers with the ones in the Learning Coach Guide.

# ASSESS

## Lesson Assessment: The French Explore America (*Online*)

Answer the online geography questions for this assessment. Your assessment will be scored by the computer.

# Student Guide
## Lesson 8: From England to America

Queen Elizabeth sparked a new spirit of patriotism among the English. They were drawn to North America by dreams of wealth and by religious ideals. Although they soon learned that colonization would not be easy, land-hungry Europeans were ready to write new chapters in the history of the Western Hemisphere.

## Lesson Objectives

- Demonstrate mastery of important knowledge and skills taught in previous lessons.
- Identify Elizabeth I as a queen of England who sponsored exploration.
- Summarize the achievements and failures of early English attempts at settlement.
- Identify the area of North America claimed by England.
- Describe England's motives for exploration and colonization as the desire to gain wealth and form model societies.
- Describe the economic and religious motives for French exploration and colonization in North America.
- Identify the area of North America claimed by the French and the routes of major explorers.
- Locate on a map the Mississippi River, Great Lakes, St. Lawrence River, Gulf of Mexico, and the Atlantic and Pacific Oceans.

## PREPARE

Approximate lesson time is 60 minutes.

### Materials

For the Student

📖 Guided Reading: Chapters 22 and 23

A History of US (Concise Edition), Volume A (Prehistory to 1800) by Joy Hakim

History Journal

## LEARN

### Activity 1: England's Attempts in the New World (Offline)

#### Instructions

#### Read

Read Chapter 22, pages 106–111, and Chapter 23, pages 112–114. Answer the questions on the Guided Reading: Chapters 22 and 23 sheet as you work. When you've finished, discuss your answers with an adult.

Use the Flash Cards to review Lessons 7 and 8 for the online assessment in this lesson.

## ASSESS

### Lesson Assessment: From England to America (Online)

You will complete an online assessment covering the main goals for Lessons 7 and 8. Your assessment will be scored by the computer.

Name _____    Date _____

## Guided Reading: Chapters 22 and 23

Read Chapters 22 and 23. Use this sheet to guide your reading and to record important facts and information.

1. Who became queen of England in 1558? _____

2. Describe England's new monarch. _____

   _____

   _____

3. What country was England most concerned about in the sixteenth century? _____

4. What were the two dreams that motivated Europeans to explore and colonize North America? _____

   _____

5. Who was the first Englishman to receive a royal charter for land in America?

   _____

6. Who wrote Utopia, and what was it about? _____

   _____

7. What favorite of Queen Elizabeth sent three expeditions to the New World?

   _____

8. What did this man name the land described by the captain of the first expedition?

   _____

9. Was the second expedition a success? Why or why not? _____

   _____

10. Describe the attitude of most Europeans toward the New World and its inhabitants.

   _____

   _____

   _____

**11.** What happened to the colony that was established on Roanoke Island in 1587?

_____

_____

**12.** Were England's early attempts at settling North America successful? Why or why not?

_____

_____

_____

# Student Guide
## Lesson 9: (Optional) Another Look

You have learned about the European exploration of North America. Now review the geography of this continent.

### Lesson Objectives
- Idenfity major geographical features and landforms of North America.

---

# PREPARE

Approximate lesson time is 60 minutes.

### Materials
For the Student

    📖 Map of North America

    A History of US (Concise Edition), Volume A (Prehistory to 1800) by Joy Hakim

    History Journal

---

# LEARN
## Activity 1. Optional: North American Geography *(Offline)*
### Instructions
### Use What You Know

Locate and label the following on the map of North America. Use a pencil. See what you can do from memory first. Use the atlas in your book as a reference as needed.

Bodies of water:

- Atlantic Ocean and Pacific Ocean
- Hudson Bay
- Great Salt Lake
- The Great Lakes
- Gulf of St. Lawrence
- Gulf of Mexico
- Caribbean Sea

---

Rivers:

- St. Lawrence
- Hudson
- Mississippi
- Missouri
- Ohio
- Rio Grande
- Colorado

Islands:

- Greenland
- Cuba
- Bahamas
- Hispaniola
- Puerto Rico

Regions/territories/places:

- Newfoundland
- Nova Scotia
- Florida
- Louisiana
- Mexico
- California

Mountain ranges (add mountain symbols):

- Rockies
- Appalachians
- Sierra Madre Occidental
- Sierra Madre Oriental
- Sierra Nevada
- Coast Ranges

# North America

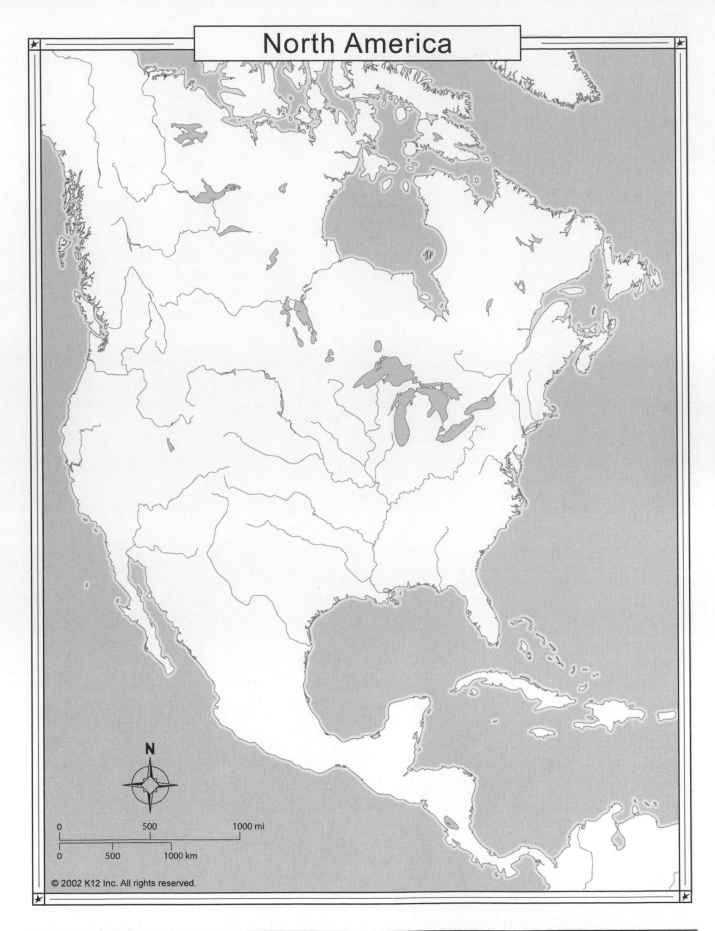

N

| 0 | 500 | 1000 mi |

| 0 | 500 | 1000 km |

# *Student Guide*
## Lesson 10: Unit Review

You've completed Unit 2, European Exploration. It's time to review what you've learned. You'll take the unit assessment in the next lesson.

### Lesson Objectives

- Demonstrate mastery of important knowledge and skills taught in previous lessons.

# PREPARE

Approximate lesson time is 60 minutes.

### Materials

> For the Student
>> A History of US (Concise Edition), Volume A (Prehistory to 1800) by Joy Hakim
>> History Journal

# LEARN
## Activity 1: A Look Back *(Offline)*
### Instructions
### Online Review

Stay online and use the following to review this unit:

- The Big Picture
- Flash Cards
- Time Line

### History Journal Review

Now, review more by going through your History Journal. Look at the sheets you completed for this unit. Review your vocabulary words. If you completed writing assignments, read them. Don't rush through. Take your time. Your History Journal is a great resource for a unit review.

# Student Guide
## Lesson 11: Unit Assessment

You've finished this unit on European exploration! Now take the Unit Assessment, and then read an assignment.

### Lesson Objectives

- Demonstrate mastery of important knowledge and skills taught in previous lessons.
- Explain the significance of new knowledge and inventions in fifteenth-century Europe, including Gutenberg's press and the compass.
- Locate the Aztec Empire on a map.
- Describe the Aztec Empire as a complex civilization.
- Identify Mesoamerica and three Mesoamerican civilizations before the Spanish conquest.
- Locate Puerto Rico, Florida, and Cuba on a map.
- Identify Francisco Vasquez de Coronado as a Spanish explorer of the southwestern United States and trace his route on a map.
- Identify Hernando de Soto as a Spanish explorer of the southeastern United States and trace on a map his route of exploration.
- Describe the behavior of the conquistadors toward the Native Americans.
- Identify one city in the United States that started as a Spanish mission.

# PREPARE

Approximate lesson time is 60 minutes.

### Materials

For the Student

- European Exploration Assessment Sheet
- A History of US (Concise Edition), Volume A (Prehistory to 1800) by Joy Hakim
- History Journal

# ASSESS

## Unit Assessment: European Exploration (*Offline*)

Complete the offline Unit Assessment. Your Learning Coach will score it and enter the results online.

# LEARN
## Activity 1: Chapters 24 and 25 *(Offline)*

### Instructions
### Read On

Who lived on the land that would one day be called Virginia? And what happened when English settlers arrived? The Woodland Indians lived well in that area. Why, then, did the English suffer from disease and starvation? Learn about both groups and what happened when English settlers arrived in 1607.

- Read Chapter 24, pages 116–120, and Chapter 25, pages 121–125.
- Prepare to compare the Powhatans and the English settlers at Jamestown.

Name _____  Date _____

# Unit Assessment

**(2 points)**
1. Explain how the printing press and the improved compass helped promote European exploration in the fifteenth century. (Write your answer in complete sentences.)

_____

_____

_____

**(2 points)**
2. Explain why fifteenth-century Europeans wanted to travel to East Asia. (Write your answer in complete sentences.)

_____

_____

_____

3. Match each person or term on the left with a description on the right. Write the correct letter on the blank line.

_____ The Vikings

_____ Christopher Columbus

_____ Moctezuma

_____ Conquistadors

_____ Columbian Exchange

_____ Elizabeth I

A. Spanish soldier-explorers

B. The movement of plants, animals, diseases, and people among continents as a result of European exploration

C. An English monarch who sponsored English exploration

D. The first Europeans to sail around the world

E. The first Europeans to make settlements in North America

F. The leader of the Aztecs

G. The first explorer to attempt to reach Asia by sailing west from Europe

Fill in the bubble in front of the correct answer.

4. What big mistake did Columbus make that led him to believe he had reached Asia?

Ⓐ He believed the Indians who told him that he had reached Asia.

Ⓑ He miscalculated the size of the earth by more than half.

Ⓒ His instruments indicated that his location was 120° W longitude.

Ⓓ He got Spanish financial and political backing.

5. Which of the following statements is true about relations between Columbus and the Native Americans?

Ⓐ Good relations turned bad when Columbus realized the Native Americans had little to offer him.

Ⓑ They enjoyed a long and prosperous trading relationship.

Ⓒ At first Columbus and the Native Americans fought, but then they made peace.

Ⓓ Columbus attacked every Native American he met.

6. African slavery was introduced to the Americas because _____.

Ⓐ the Native American population was reduced and African slaves were needed to work the sugar plantations

Ⓑ the Spanish conquered Africa and took millions of Africans as slaves

Ⓒ the Spanish needed a large army to defeat the Native Americans, and African slaves were immune to New World diseases

Ⓓ a potato famine in Africa forced millions of starving Africans into slavery

7. Which of these is a true statement about the Aztecs and the Spanish?

Ⓐ The Aztecs defeated the Spanish in battle and made them pay tribute in gold.

Ⓑ The Aztecs allowed the Spanish to build forts as bases for exploration in exchange for guns and horses.

Ⓒ The Aztecs had a secret city called Cíbola, where they hid from the Spanish for more than a century.

Ⓓ The Aztecs had a complex civilization that was destroyed by the Spanish conquerors.

8. Cortés, de Soto, Ponce de León, and Coronado explored for which country?

   (A) England

   (B) France

   (C) Portugal

   (D) Spain

9. Which of these statements about the behavior of the conquistadors toward the Native Americans is **FALSE**?

   (A) The conquistadors robbed, enslaved, and killed Native Americans.

   (B) The conquistadors believed it was their duty to convert Native Americans to Christianity.

   (C) The conquistadors paid tribute to the Native Americans in exchange for safe passage through their lands.

   (D) The conquistadors viewed the Native American lands as theirs for the taking.

10. Which of these cities in the United States was started as a Spanish mission?

    (A) Santa Fe

    (B) Dallas

    (C) Tampa

    (D) Las Vegas

11. Which of these statements was not a reason for French exploration and colonization in North America?

    (A) The French wanted to enslave the Native Americans and bring them back to France for labor.

    (B) The French wanted to find a northwest sea passage to get to Asia.

    (C) French Huguenots came to escape religious persecution in France.

    (D) The French wanted to look for gold and set up trading posts for fur trappers and fishermen.

**12.** Which of the following statements regarding English settlement in North America before 1600 is true?

(A) The first English settlements in North America were all successful.

(B) Half of the first English settlements in North America were successful and half were failures.

(C) All of the early English attempts at settlement in North America were failures.

(D) The English weren't interested in settlements in North America; they wanted to find a northwest passage to Asia.

*(2 points)*
**13.** Describe at least two reasons for English exploration and colonization in North America. (Write your answer in complete sentences.)

_____

_____

_____

Refer to this map for the following questions.

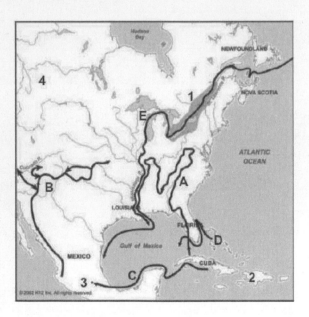

Place the number from the map that matches the place.

**14.** _____ Aztec Empire

**15.** _____ New France

Place the letter from the map that matches the route taken by an explorer or explorers.

**16.** _____ Cortés

**17.** _____ de Soto

**18.** _____ Ponce de León

**19.** _____ Coronado

**20.** _____ the collective routes taken by the French explorers Cartier, Champlain, Marquetteand Joliet, and La Salle

# *Student Guide*
## Lesson 1: A Beginning in Virginia

English businessmen wanted to make money by sending settlers to Virginia to find gold. There was no gold, and disease and starvation killed most of the early settlers. But in time they did make money âby raising tobacco. A few years later, Pilgrims arrived on shores to the north, looking for a place to practice their religion. Puritans followed, and New England grew.

A Woodland Indian culture thrived on the land that would be called Virginia. This well-organized Indian culture consisted of hunters and farmers. When English settlers arrived they faced troubles from the start. The Indians attacked them. Their settlement was in a poor location. They faced disease and starvation.

### Lesson Objectives

- Locate the Chesapeake Bay, the James River, and Jamestown on a map.
- Assess the needs of a group of settlers in a new place and list the kinds of people and equipment needed for success, including builders, doctors, and farmers.
- Describe the men and boys who sailed for Jamestown as gentlemen unprepared for hard work, their motivation as their desire for gold, and the difficulties they faced such as disease, starvation, and poor location and leadership.
- Explain that the Powhatans were able to live well by hunting, fishing, and farming the great resources of Virginia, while the early English settlers suffered because of poor planning and lack of skills.

---

# PREPARE

Approximate lesson time is 60 minutes.

### Materials

For the Student

📇 Map of Early American Settlements

A History of US (Concise Edition), Volume A (Prehistory to 1800) by Joy Hakim

History Journal

---

# LEARN
## Activity 1: Virginia Settlements *(Offline)*
### Instructions
Check Your Reading (Chapter 24, pages 116-120, and Chapter 25, pages 121-125)

The first Virginians were Woodland Indians who hunted, fished, farmed, and fought in a region of great abundance. But their lives changed dramatically with the arrival of English settlers.

---

In your History Journal, write "Powhatans" at the top of the page, "English Settlers" one-third of the way down, and "Both" at the two-thirds mark. Then write the following phrases under the name of the group or groups they describe. Check your answers with an adult.

- Arrived by ship
- Searched for gold
- Lived in dozens of villages in eastern Virginia
- Hunted deer and raised vegetables
- Spent too little time planning and planting
- Settled in a swampy area
- Men hunted, fished, and fought; women farmed
- Waged war on enemies
- Used bear grease to ward off mosquitoes
- Ate berries, grapes, and seafood

## Discuss

Use the map of Early American Settlements to discuss the following:

- Locate Jamestown on the map. What river is it on? Describe the location of this river.
- What larger body of water brought the settlers to the Chesapeake Bay?

## Read On

John Smith was a tough leader. Not everyone liked him, but he led the colonists through their first months in Jamestown.

Read Chapter 26, pages, 126-130, and Chapter 27, pages 131-133. Before you read, think about how you might have handled the lazy, unskilled settlers at Jamestown. What do you think could have happened to cause a "starving time"? Write your thoughts in your History Journal.

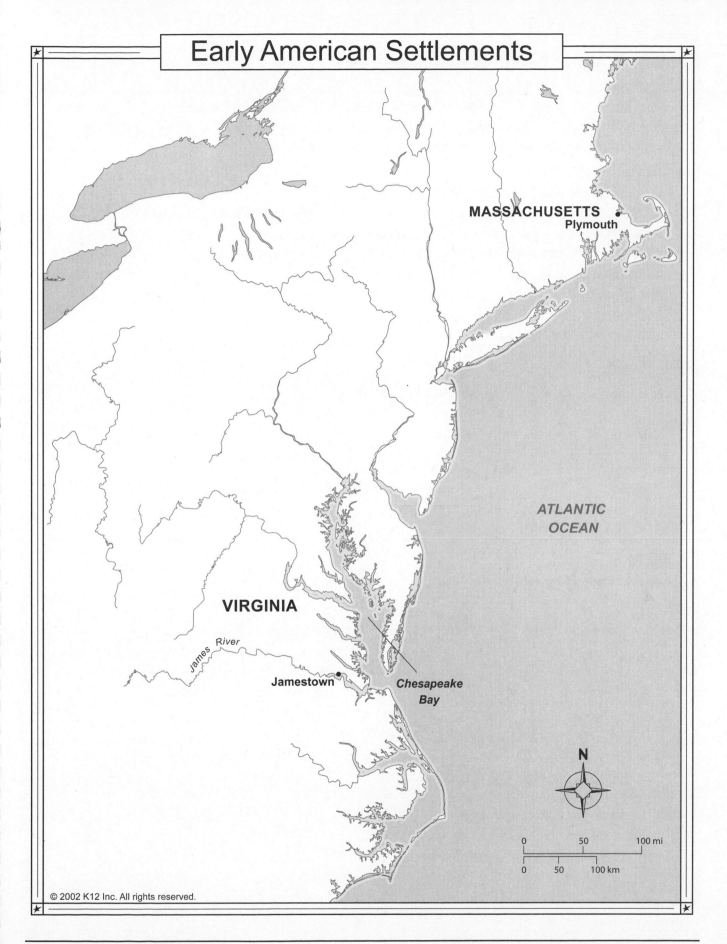

# Early American Settlements

MASSACHUSETTS
Plymouth

ATLANTIC
OCEAN

VIRGINIA

James River

Jamestown

Chesapeake
Bay

N

| 0 | | 50 | | 100 mi |
| 0 | | 50 | | 100 km |

# *Student Guide*
## Lesson 2: John Smith and Jamestown

John Smith was a tough leader. He dealt with the local Indians. He dealt with the settlers, too. He pulled the colony through its first faltering months. But the winter of 1609-1610 almost wiped Jamestown out. The settlers ran out of food. Starvation shrank the settlement from 500 men to just 60.

### Lesson Objectives
- Summarize the story of John Smith.
- Identify adjectives to describe John Smith, and explain the reasons he was able to save the colony, including his work policy and relationship with the Indians.
- Identify Pocahontas as the daughter of the chief Powhatan, and compare fictional accounts of her with historical fact.
- Explain how the Jamestown colony was saved from extinction when English ships arrived after a starving time.

---

# PREPARE

Approximate lesson time is 60 minutes.

### Materials
For the Student
- The Settlers Settle
- A History of US (Concise Edition), Volume A (Prehistory to 1800) by Joy Hakim
- History Journal

---

# LEARN
## Activity 1: Pocahontas Plus *(Offline)*
### Instructions
**Check Your Reading (Chapter 26, pages 126-130, and Chapter 27, pages, 131-133)**

When you read Chapters 26 and 27, you probably noticed a familiar name--Pocahontas. How did what you read compare with what you already knew?

Which of these statements are true and which are false?

1. Pocahontas was an Indian princess.
2. She saved John Smith's life twice.
3. She was about 12 years old when the settlers arrived.
4. Her father wanted her to marry John Smith.
5. Powhatan was Pocahontas's father.

**Use What You Know**

The Starving Time

In your History Journal, record background information--who, what, when, where, why, and how--that a reporter would need to write an article on the Starving Time. Discuss your answers with an adult.

The Biography of Captain John Smith

Suppose you wanted to write a biography of Captain John Smith. How would you organize your information?

The Settlers Settle page will help you think about and organize the important information you would need. Answer all the questions. Have an adult check your answers.

**Read On**

What does tobacco have to do with silk? Nothing now, but it did in the early history of Jamestown.

Read Chapter 28, pages 134-136, and Chapter 29, pages 137-141. Think about the things that happened in Virginia that year. List the three things you think are most important.

Vocabulary

You'll see these terms as you read. Write a brief definition for each term as you come to it.

- burgess
- colony
- indentured servant
- slave

Name _____    Date _____

**Bio Facts** Suppose that you want to write a biography of Captain John Smith. Before you begin writing, you have to organize some of the important information that you need. Fill in what you've learned below.

### About Jamestown

1. What business group sent the Englishmen to Virginia in 1607? _____

2. What were the Englishmen looking for? _____

   _____

3. Why didn't the settlers want to work? _____

   _____

4. What was good and bad about Jamestown's location? _____

   _____

### About John Smith

5. Why was John Smith in chains when the ships arrived in Virginia? _____

   _____

6. How did Smith get the settlers to work? _____

   _____

7. What did Smith trade with the Indians? _____

8. Why did the Indians respect John Smith? _____

   _____

9. What did John Smith think about America? _____

   _____

## Writing the Biography

**10.** You have to give your biography a title. Chose one of the following titles and circle it. Why do you think yours is the better title? Why didn't you choose the other one? You may write your answer on the back of this sheet.

- Captain John Smith, Brave and Smart
- John Smith, the Most Popular Man in Jamestown

**Thinking Cap Question!** What if Powhatan were writing a biography of John Smith? What would he say? In your History Journal, write a paragraph that Powhatan might have written about the new white leader.

# *Student Guide*
## Lesson 3: Tobacco and Turning Points

The Virginia colonists did not find riches in gold. They found them in tobacco! The colony needed workers. Indentured servants, and then slaves, were brought in to fill that need. The year 1619 marked three important events in the course of American life: (1) The first boatload of Englishwomen arrived in Virginia. (2) The English colonies in America became permanent and the people gained important rights. (3) African workers were brought to Virginia. This led to centuries of slavery.

### Lesson Objectives
- Identify the role of tobacco in the economic success of Jamestown.
- Explain the beginnings of slavery in Virginia as a way to fill the need for field workers, and the difference between an indentured servant and a slave.
- Describe the significance of the Virginia Charter in guaranteeing the rights of Englishmen to all settlers of the Jamestown colony.
- Identify the House of Burgesses as the first representative assembly in the European colonies.

# PREPARE

Approximate lesson time is 60 minutes.

### Materials
For the Student

A History of US (Concise Edition), Volume A (Prehistory to 1800) by Joy Hakim

History Journal

paper, construction, 9" x 12"

pencils, colored, 16 colors or more

### Keywords and Pronunciation
**stygian** (STIH-jee-uhn)

# LEARN
## Activity 1: What Doesn't Belong? *(Offline)*
### Instructions
**Check Your Reading (Chapter 28, pages 134–136, and Chapter 29, pages 137–141)**

What doesn't belong? Read each numbered word or phrase. Then read the phrases underneath. Figure out which phrase does not belong in each group. Check your answers with an adult.

1. tobacco

- hated by King James
- not very profitable
- required a lot of workers to grow
- new variety developed by John Rolfe

2. indentured servants

- worked from four to seven years for freedom
- some were criminals
- some were treated like slaves
- called that because of bad teeth

3. boatload of Africans

- first came to Virginia on a Dutch ship
- immediately became slaves forever
- some owned their own land
- originally treated like indentured servants

4. House of Burgesses

- a group of lawmakers first elected in 1619
- an assembly in Virginia like Parliament in England
- a huge plantation home belonging originally to the Burgesses
- America's first representative government

## Use What You Know

King James used some strong words to describe how he felt about tobacco. Read the quotation in the sidebar on page 135 aloud. Ask for help with any words you don't understand. Or listen to someone else reading it aloud. Can you almost hear King James talking?

Now create an anti-tobacco advertisement for the king. Reread what he had to say about tobacco before you begin.

## Read On

The colonists and the Indians went from good intentions to violent conflict. Why do you think this happened?

Read Chapter 30, pages 142–145. Before you begin reading, predict the answer to the first of these questions. Then read to see if you were right. Answer the second question in your History Journal.

1. What was the major reason that the Europeans and Indians had no hope of living in peace with each other?
2. What factors in England helped Jamestown succeed?

# Student Guide
## Lesson 4: Conflict

Conflict was brewing between the Europeans and the Indians. The Europeans wanted to control more land. The Indians knew that losing land would destroy their way of life. The conflict soon became violent. Still, more people arrived from England. Slavery increased as well.

## Lesson Objectives

- Identify James I as the king of England at the time Virginia was settled.
- Describe the factors in England that pushed people to come to America, including poverty and a growing population.
- Explain the reasons for conflict between English settlers and Native Americans as racism and the disagreement over land use and ownership.
- Explain that slavery had existed in Africa long before slavery came to America but that there were major differences.

---

# PREPARE

Approximate lesson time is 60 minutes.

## Materials

For the Student

🖥 Act 1: Jamestown

A History of US (Concise Edition), Volume A (Prehistory to 1800) by Joy Hakim

History Journal

🖥 Conflict Assessment Sheet

---

# LEARN
## Activity 1: Indians vs. English (Offline)
### Instructions
**Check Your Reading (Chapter 30, pages 142–145)**

Talk over the following with an adult:

1. Did you predict what happened in Chapter 30? Don't worry if you didn't—predictions can't always be right.
2. What was the main reason for conflict between English settlers and Native Americans?
3. How did the Great Massacre of 1622 lead to more violence?
4. Why were people leaving England to settle in Virginia?
5. King James thought he was absolutely divine and always right. King James also thought he ruled by "divine right," which is different. What is divine right?
6. Before the first African slaves were brought to America, slavery had existed for a long time. Where? When? How? What happened in America to make slavery develop into "a terrible and degrading system"?

---

**Use What You Know**

Complete the Act I: Jamestown sheet and see if you think history is like a play. Check your answers with an adult.

**Read On**

Read Chapter 31, pages 146–150, and Chapter 32, pages 151–155. Look for the answers to these questions as you read.

1. Who were the Saints?
2. Who were the Strangers?
3. What was a Puritan?
4. Who was Squanto?

Look for these things and people, too. Write something about each of them in your History Journal.

- Pilgrim
- Mayflower
- William Bradford
- Constitution
- Mayflower Compact

---

# ASSESS

## Lesson Assessment: Conflict (*Offline*)

You will complete an offline assessment covering the main goals for the lesson. An adult will score the assessment and enter the results online.

Name _____     Date _____

## Act 1: Jamestown

Some people say that history is like a play. There is a setting—a place such as Jamestown. There is a time—such as the early 1600s. And there is a cast of characters—the people who take part in the events, whose lives are the real story of history. Answer these questions as if you were a member in the cast of characters at Jamestown. Use the back of this sheet if necessary.

You are a woman from England. It is 1619:

1. Why did you come to Jamestown? _____

_____

2. What are some of the ways you would like to change Jamestown? _____

_____

_____

You are a burgess. It is 1619:

3. What is your job? _____

4. In what way is the House of Burgesses a "first"? _____

_____

You are an African. It is 1619:

5. How and why were you taken from your home? _____

_____

6. How did the African slave trade start? _____

_____

You are a Powhatan Indian. It is 1622:

7. Do you and the Europeans disagree about land? Why? _____

_____

Adapted from *A History of US*

8. The Europeans are Christian. How do they view your people and your beliefs?

_____

_____

9. What did some of your people do in March 1622? _____

_____

**Thinking Cap Question!** The play is entitled "Jamestown Days." Of the above characters, which one would you most like to be? In your History Journal, either write one scene that involves your character or draw a picture of your character. If you need help, refer to your book. It contains many details about the everyday life of various Jamestown dwellers.

Name            Date

## Lesson Assessment

**Word Wise** Define each of these terms in a complete sentence:

**1.** indentured servant

_____

**2.** arrogance

_____

**3.** divine right

_____

**Big Changes** How did each of these people, things, or events change Jamestown? Please use complete sentences for your answers.

**4.** tobacco

_____

_____

**5.** Africans

_____

_____

**6.** the House of Burgesses

_____

_____

**7.** poverty in England

_____

_____

# Student Guide
## Lesson 5: Pilgrims and Promises

A group of people in England was unhappy with the established church. They no longer wanted to be part of it. First they fled to Holland. Then, in 1620, the Pilgrims settled in America. They struggled through their first year because they arrived after the planting season was over. The Indians helped them. Meanwhile, times grew harder for another religious group in England—the Puritans.

### Lesson Objectives
- Describe the goals of the Separatists, or Pilgrims, including religious freedom.
- Describe the Mayflower Compact as an early form of self-government in Plymouth and William Bradford as the governor.
- Identify Squanto as an Indian who taught the Pilgrims how to survive in their new home.
- Describe the hardships faced by the Pilgrims, including starvation and cold.

---

# PREPARE

Approximate lesson time is 60 minutes.

### Materials
For the Student

📖 A Land of Differences Activity Sheet

A History of US (Concise Edition), Volume A (Prehistory to 1800) by Joy Hakim

History Journal

---

# LEARN
## Activity 1: Strangers, Saints, and Pilgrims (Offline)
### Instructions
Check Your Reading (Chapter 31, pages 146–150, and Chapter 32, pages 151–155)

You read about many people, ideas, and adventures in Chapters 31 and 32. The Land of Differences sheet will help you sort them out. After you answer each question, turn the paper over and write down the reason behind your choice.

For the Thinking Cap Question, write a caption for the picture. Be sure to look carefully at the picture and think about what it means.

---

## Use What You Know

Imagine that you were a Pilgrim—one who kept a diary. Write three short diary entries in your History Journal. Each entry should describe one of the following:

- problems in the trip, or life in the new colony
- the way the settlement was governed
- the help the Indians gave, especially Squanto

## Read On

In 1630 the first Puritans arrived in the New World. What do you remember about the Puritans and what they wanted to do?

Read Chapter 33, pages 156–158, and Chapter 34, pages 159–163. Predict the answers to the following questions and write them in your History Journal. Check them and change them as you read.

1.  How is a charter like a constitution?
2.  What did toleration mean to the Puritans?
3.  Why did the Puritans dislike the Quakers?
4.  What does *theocracy* mean?
5.  What was the *common* in a Puritan village?
6.  What did the Puritans think about education?

# ASSESS

## Lesson Assessment: Pilgrims and Promises (*Online*)

You will complete an online assessment covering the main goals of this lesson. Your assessment will be scored by the computer.

Name _____     Date _____

## A Land of Differences

Different Ideas, Different Ways When the Pilgrims and Puritans came to America, they brought many different customs and ideas. Read each statement below. Circle the name of the person or group who might have said it.

1. "My church is the established church in England."

   a Roman Catholic                            an Anglican

2. "We believe that we can worship God on our own, without priests."

   Catholics                            Separatists

3. "I am unhappy in England and hope to find a life of adventure in America."

   a Saint                            a Stranger

4. "We want to build a perfect society."

   Pilgrims                            indentured servants

5. "I will tell the story of the Pilgrims."

   William Bradford                            John Winthrop

6. "My people agree to a peace treaty with the Pilgrims."

   Powhatan                            Massasoit

The Pilgrims' ideas about government were different from King James's ideas. Answer the following questions about the Pilgrims' form of government:

7. The Pilgrims agreed to live together under a government of laws. The document they

   signed is called: _____

8. Why do you think this document is considered one of the great documents of American

   history?_____

   _____

**Thinking Cap Question!** Write a caption for this picture.

Adapted from *A History of US*

# Student Guide
## Lesson 6: What's a Puritan?

In 1630, Puritans began the Massachusetts Bay Colony. They set up a new government there. Now they were free to follow their own religious beliefs. But they did not accept other religions. New England villages were well planned. They had places for living, working, and teaching. They had places for worship and for public meetings.

## Lesson Objectives

- Define *Puritan* and describe the problems Puritans faced in England, including religious persecution.
- Describe the Puritan settlement of Massachusetts Bay, including the colony's charter, leadership, and religious policy.
- Explain the importance of education to the Puritans as the need to read the Bible, and give examples of the kinds of education established in Massachusetts Bay, including town schools and Harvard College.
- Describe the towns in Massachusetts Bay.

# PREPARE

Approximate lesson time is 60 minutes.

## Materials

For the Student

📖 Puritan Life Activity Sheet

A History of US (Concise Edition), Volume A (Prehistory to 1800) by Joy Hakim

History Journal

# LEARN
## Activity 1: Puritans and More Puritans *(Offline)*
### Instructions
**Check Your Reading (Chapter 33, pages 156–158, and Chapter 34, pages 159–163)**

- Complete the Puritan Life sheet.
- Ask an adult to check your answers.

**Use What You Know**

Draw a map of your own New England town. Include:

- A New England setting
- At least three of the most important buildings in a New England town
- The commons
- A name for the town

Name _____    Date _____

# Puritan Life

By 1640, 20,000 Puritans had come to New England. When they settled, they adopted many new customs and incorporated changes in their daily lives. Write a sentence to explain how each of the following things or places was part of Puritan life in America.

**1.** the Charter: _____

_____

**2.** religious freedom: _____

_____

**3.** ministers: _____

_____

**4.** stockades: _____

_____

**5.** the meetinghouse: _____

_____

**6.** the common: _____

_____

**7.** Harvard College: _____

_____

**8.** schoolteachers: _____

_____

**9.** sermons: _____

_____

Adapted from *A History of US*

# *Student Guide*
## Lesson 7: Waterways or Waterwheels

There were big differences between life in Jamestown and life in Massachusetts. One reason for the differences was geography.

### Lesson Objectives
- Analyze the geography of the eastern seaboard of the United States.
- Predict economic activity based on the geography of a region.

---

# PREPARE

Approximate lesson time is 60 minutes.

### Materials

For the Student

    📖 Collecting Evidence

    📖 Map of U.S. Fall Line

    History Journal

---

# LEARN
## Activity 1: Geography Makes a Difference *(Offline)*
### Instructions
### Waterfalls and Waterways

Imagine traveling in a boat up a river. If you started where the river meets the ocean, or the mouth of the river, what would happen when you got near a waterfall? Could you continue going up the river?
The waterfall is there because there is a steep drop in the elevation of the land. The river falls from the higher elevation to the lower. If you step out of your boat onto the shore and try to walk, you will find yourself climbing from rock to rock—moving into the mountains where the river started.

In colonial times, there were very few roads and no tunnels in North America. Most people stopped going inland when they came to a waterfall. It was just too hard to go any farther. And the rocky, hilly land just beyond the waterfalls was not very good for farming. Usually people stayed between the Atlantic Ocean and the foothills, or beginnings, of the Appalachian Mountains. This area is called a coastal plain. If the mountains are far from the ocean there can be a very wide coastal plain. But if the mountains are close to the ocean there may be no coastal plain at all. The land in the Chesapeake is very different from the land in New England. So is the climate. Geography is one reason life was so different in the two regions.

---

Use the map of the U.S. Fall Line and answer these questions in your History Journal.

1. How many miles wide is the coastal plain near the Virginia-North Carolina border at the southernmost end of the Chesapeake Bay? Use the scale shown on the map and a ruler to measure the coastal plain, shown in dark gray on the map.

2. How wide is the coastal plain (the dark gray area) on the mainland of Massachusetts?

3. Look at the location of the waterfalls in Massachusetts and Virginia. Find them by matching the symbol in the map key to the map itself. What do you think the land is like in the area between the coastal plain and the mountains? This area is shown in light gray on the onscreen map. Remember what causes a waterfall. Is the land in that area likely to be flat or hilly? Smooth or rocky?

4. Look at the direction in which the rivers flow. Remember, rivers always flow toward a larger body of water such as a bay or an ocean. If you floated on a river in Virginia, in what direction would you go?

5. If you floated on most rivers in New England, in what direction would you go?

6. If you wanted to travel a long way west from the ocean on a river, would you choose to do it in Virginia or Massachusetts? Why?

7. If you wanted to pack your belongings and move far away from your neighbors on the coast, would it be easier in Massachusetts or Virginia?

8. Now think about how people might live in the two regions. If you wanted to have a big farm with thousands of acres and many workers, would you settle in Virginia or Massachusetts? Why?

9. If you wanted to live in a town with close neighbors and other towns nearby, would you settle in Virginia or Massachusetts? Why?

10. Water is powerful. It can turn waterwheels that move other wheels for energy. If you wanted to build a waterwheel that had a lot of waterpower to turn it, would you build it near or far from a waterfall? Why?

## Use What You Know

Some early settlers had trouble finding a good way to earn a living. They could have used advice from someone who knew the geography of the region.

The king wants to know how to make the colonies successful. He knows it was a mistake for settlers in Jamestown to spend their time looking for gold.

Here is the scenario for your assignment. Pretend to be an adviser to the king. Write a letter to him suggesting what the colonists in Virginia should do. Then describe what economic activities the settlers in Massachusetts should consider. Use the Collecting Evidence sheet to help you organize your information.

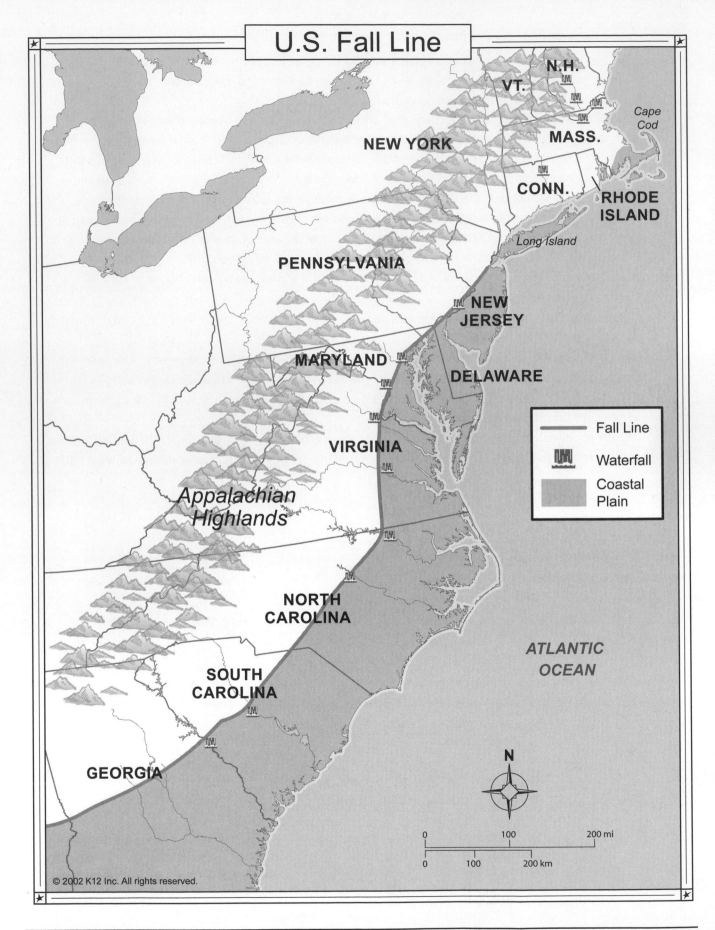

# U.S. Fall Line

N.H.
VT.
MASS.
NEW YORK
CONN.
RHODE ISLAND
*Cape Cod*
*Long Island*
PENNSYLVANIA
NEW JERSEY
MARYLAND
DELAWARE
VIRGINIA
*Appalachian Highlands*
NORTH CAROLINA
ATLANTIC OCEAN
SOUTH CAROLINA
GEORGIA

| | Fall Line |
| --- | --- |
| | Waterfall |
| | Coastal Plain |

N

| 0 | 100 | 200 mi |
| 0 | 100 | 200 km |

© 2002 K12 Inc. All rights reserved.

Name _____     Date _____

## Collecting Evidence

Refer to the map of the U.S. Fall Line and use what you have learned in earlier lessons to answer the following questions. When you are finished, compare your answers with those found in the Learning Coach Guide.

1. List three ways geography influences what kinds of work people do.

   _____

   _____

   _____

   _____

2. Describe the geography of New England. Include the land, rivers, and climate.

   _____

   _____

   _____

   _____

   _____

3. Suggest economic activities that will be successful in New England.

   _____

   _____

   _____

   _____

   _____

4. Describe the geography of Virginia. Include the land, rivers, and climate.

_____

_____

_____

_____

_____

5. Suggest economic activities that will be successful in Virginia.

_____

_____

_____

_____

_____

# *Student Guide*
## Lesson 8: (Optional) Thankful for Feasting

### Lesson Objectives
- Explore the history and traditions of Thanksgiving.

## PREPARE

Approximate lesson time is 60 minutes.

## LEARN
### Activity 1. Optional: A Plymouth Celebration *(Online)*
### Instructions
Go online to the Plimoth Plantation's "You Are the Historian" activity and learn more about the American Thanksgiving tradition (http://www.plimoth.org/education/olc/index_js2.html).

# *Student Guide*
## Lesson 9: Unit Review

You have completed Unit 3, Thirteen Colonies, Part 1. It's time to review what you've learned. You'll take the Unit Assessment in the next lesson.

### Lesson Objectives
- Review early English settlement in North America.

---

# PREPARE

Approximate lesson time is 60 minutes.

### Materials
For the Student

A History of US (Concise Edition), Volume A (Prehistory to 1800) by Joy Hakim

History Journal

---

# LEARN
## Activity 1: A Look Back *(Offline)*
### Instructions
#### Online Review

Go online and use the following to review this unit:

- The Big Picture
- Flash Cards
- Time Line

#### History Journal Review

Review some more by going through your History Journal. Look at the activity sheets you completed for this unit. Review your vocabulary words. If you completed any writing assignments, read them. Don't rush through; take your time. Your History Journal is a great resource for a unit review.

---

# Student Guide
## Lesson 10: Unit Assessment

You've finished this unit. Take the unit assessment. Then take a break!

## Lesson Objectives

- Demonstrate mastery of important knowledge and skills taught in previous lessons.
- Locate the Chesapeake Bay, the James River, and Jamestown on a map.
- Describe the men and boys who sailed for Jamestown as gentlemen unprepared for hard work, their motivation as their desire for gold, and the difficulties they faced such as disease, starvation, and poor location and leadership.
- Explain how the Jamestown colony was saved from extinction when English ships arrived after a starving time.
- Identify the role of tobacco in the economic success of Jamestown.
- Explain the beginnings of slavery in Virginia as a way to fill the need for field workers, and the difference between an indentured servant and a slave.
- Describe the Mayflower Compact as an early form of self-government in Plymouth and William Bradford as the governor.
- Describe the Puritan settlement of Massachusetts Bay, including the colony's charter, leadership, and religious policy.
- Explain the importance of education to the Puritans as the need to read the Bible, and give examples of the kinds of education established in Massachusetts Bay, including town schools and Harvard College.
- Analyze the geography of the eastern seaboard of the United States.
- Predict economic activity based on the geography of a region.
- Describe the significance of the Virginia Charter in guaranteeing the rights of Englishmen to all settlers of the Jamestown colony.
- Identify the House of Burgesses as the first representative assembly in the European colonies.
- Identify James I as the king of England at the time Virginia was settled.
- Describe the factors in England that pushed people to come to America, including poverty and a growing population.
- Explain the reasons for conflict between English settlers and Native Americans as racism and the disagreement over land use and ownership.
- Describe the hardships faced by the Pilgrims, including starvation and cold.
- Describe the Puritan settlement of Massachusetts Bay, including the colony's charter, leadership, and religious policy.
- Explain the importance of education to the Puritans as the need to read the Bible, and give examples of the kinds of education established in Massachusetts Bay, including town schools and Harvard College.

# PREPARE

Approximate lesson time is 60 minutes.

## Materials

For the Student

🖳 Thirteen Colonies, Part 1 Assessment Sheet

---

# ASSESS

## Unit Assessment: Thirteen Colonies, Part 1 (*Offline*)

Complete the offline Unit Assessment. Your Learning Coach will score it and enter the results online.

Name _____ Date _____

# Unit Assessment

1. Match each term on the left with its description on the right. Write the correct letter on the line in front of the term.

   _____ Virginia Charter

   _____ Mayflower Compact

   _____ Harvard College

   _____ House of Burgesses

   **A.** first representative assembly in the European colonies

   **B.** guaranteed the rights of Englishmen to all settlers of the Jamestown Colony

   **C.** an early form of self-government in Plymouth

   **D.** school founded by the Puritans

2. Which of these best describes most of the early Jamestown settlers?

   (A) laborers used to hard work

   (B) gentlemen unprepared for hard work

   (C) farmers with skills to raise crops

   (D) soldiers prepared to fight the Indians

3. Which of these was most important to the economic success of Jamestown?

   (A) cotton

   (B) silk

   (C) corn

   (D) tobacco

4. The beginnings of slavery in Virginia can be explained as a way to fill the need for _____ .

   (A) craftsmen

   (B) field workers

   (C) soldiers

   (D) gold miners

5. Which two of these were the main factors that caused large numbers of people to leave England and go to America? (Select both correct answers.)

   (A) interest in exploration

   (B) widespread poverty

   (C) desire for adventure

   (D) a growing population

6. Why was education so important to the Puritans?

   (A) so that people could become farmers

   (B) so that people could read newspapers

   (C) so that people could write home to England

   (D) so that people could read the Bible

7. Give two reasons why the Eastern Woodland Indians were able to live well and two reasons why the early settlers had so many problems.

   _____

   _____

   _____

   _____

8. Complete this chart using the words and phrases from the word box below. Use each word or phrase only once. Only one word or phrase will go in each box. Three have been filled in for you.

| Colony | Locations | Climate | Settlers | Goals | Leadership | Achievements and Failures |
|---|---|---|---|---|---|---|
| **Jamestown** | | | | | | |
| **Plymouth** | | very cold winters | | | | |
| **Massachusetts Bay** | New England | | | | John Winthrop | |

| | | | | |
|---|---|---|---|---|
| John Smith | Separatists | public education | near Cape Cod | New England |
| cold and windy | religious freedom | William Bradford | near Chesapeake Bay | |
| Mayflower Compact | hot summers/cold winters | Puritans | Starving Time | |
| purify Church of England | gentlemen adventrers | find gold | | |

**9.** The Puritans were very tolerant. They let people who practiced other religions settle in their communities.

(A) True

(B) False

**10.** There was always cooperation between Native Americans and the early colonists.

(A) True

(B) False

**11.** The Pilgrims survived their first winter without help from the Indians.

(A) True

(B) False

**12.** There were a lot of problems between the Native Americans and the colonists. What was the main problem?

(A) differences in religion

(B) use of the land

(C) inability to communicate

(D) growing trade

**13.** Life on the Chesapeake and life in New England were very different. What was a major reason for the difference?

(A) animals

(B) geography

(C) education

(D) weather

**14.** Virginia's _____ and the Pilgrim's _____ were the beginnings of representative government in the colonies.

**15.** Which region has a wider coastal plain, New England or Virginia? _____

16. Towns and small farms developed in New England. Large plantations and very few towns developed in Virginia. Give at least four reasons for this.

_____

_____

_____

_____

17. Who was king of England when Jamestown and Plymouth were first being settled?

_____

18. Label these places on the map.
   • Jamestown
   • James River
   • Chesapeake Bay

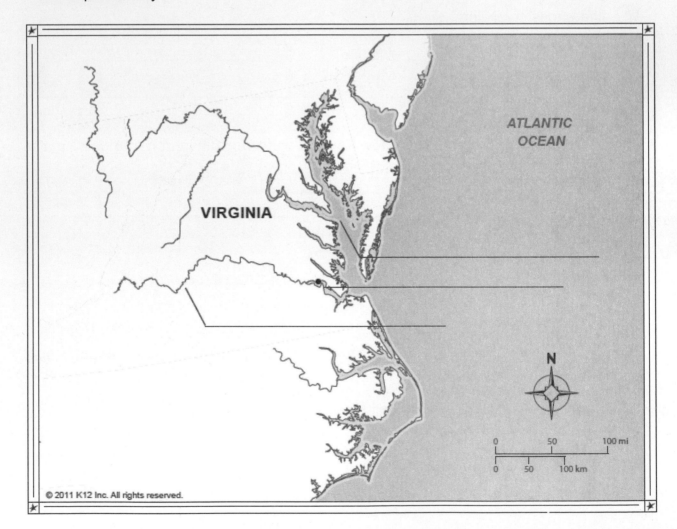

# Student Guide
## Lesson 1: Breaks with Tradition: Roger Williams

Geography and values both play a big part in the way people live. In the southern colonies, good soil and warm weather led to the growth of plantations. In New England, towns and industry grew near fast rivers and the coast. The middle colonies had both cities and farms. Different kinds of people lived there, many of them tolerant of other religions.

Roger Williams was a Puritan minister with some non-Puritan ideas and beliefs. Williams's beliefs led to the founding of a new colony. Some of his ideas are central to American life even today.

## Lesson Objectives

- Identify Roger Williams as the founder of Rhode Island and a supporter of religious toleration and fair treatment of Native Americans.
- Explain the advantages of relative location to natural harbors in the settlement of Providence.
- Locate the colony of Rhode Island on a map and list its founder, his motives, and his accomplishments.

# PREPARE

Approximate lesson time is 60 minutes.

## Materials

For the Student

🖳 The Thirteen Colonies

A History of US (Concise Edition), Volume A (Prehistory to 1800) by Joy Hakim

History Journal

# LEARN
## Activity 1: Roger Williams (Offline)
### Instructions
### Read

You've learned that the Separatists and the Puritans had been involved with religious conflicts in England. The Separatists wanted to separate themselves from the Church of England, and the Puritans wanted to purify the Church of England. As a result of these conflicts new colonies were founded in North America. Now you will meet a man who had religious conflicts with the Puritans from the Massachusetts Bay Colony. These religious conflicts lead to the founding of another new colony. In today's reading you will learn about Roger Williams and how his ideas and beliefs led to the founding of a new colony.

Read Chapter 35, pages 164–167. As you read, prepare to discuss the answers to these questions:

1. Who was Roger Williams?
2. How did his beliefs differ from traditional Puritan beliefs?
3. How did these beliefs lead to the founding of a new colony?

4. What was the new colony called?
5. Was there conflict or cooperation between this new colony and the Native Americans?

Vocabulary

You'll see these terms as you read. Write a brief definition for each term in your History Journal.

- freedom of conscience
- atheist (AY-thee-ist)
- separation of church and state

## Check Your Reading (Chapter 35, pages 164–167)

Discuss Chapter 35 with an adult.

## Use What You Know

- Locate and label Rhode Island and Providence on the map on the Thirteen Colonies sheet.
- Complete the section in the chart for Rhode Island.
- In your History Journal, explain why Williams might have chosen the geographic location of the new colony. Explain his motive for establishing the new colony, and list the colony's accomplishments.

## Read On

You learned how the Puritans banished Roger Williams from the Massachusetts Bay Colony because of religious conflict. Williams founded the Rhode Island colony and allowed others to practice the religion of their choice. But religious conflict in Massachusetts Bay did not stop after Roger Williams was banished. Anne Hutchinson and Mary Dyer were two women who broke with Puritan religious beliefs and practices.

Read Chapter 36, pages 168–171. As you read, think about how the beliefs of Anne Hutchinson and Mary Dyer were different from the beliefs of most Puritans.

Vocabulary

You'll see these terms as you read. Write a brief definition for each as you come to it.

- chattel
- Quaker
- divine right of kings
- martyr

Name            Date

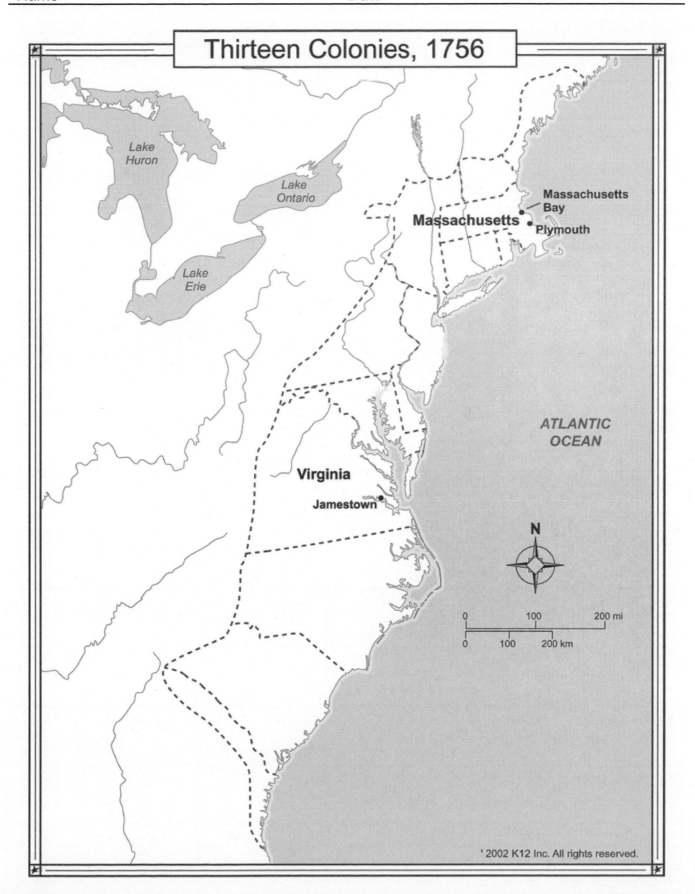

Thirteen Colonies, 1756

Lake Huron

Lake Ontario

Lake Erie

Massachusetts Bay

Massachusetts

Plymouth

ATLANTIC OCEAN

Virginia

Jamestown

N

| 0 | 100 | 200 mi |
| 0 | 100 | 200 km |

' 2002 K12 Inc. All rights reserved.

| Colony | Date Founded | Founder(s) |
|---|---|---|
| New Hampshire | 1680 | |
| Massachusetts | Plymouth: 1620 | Pilgrims |
| | Massachusetts Bay Colony: 1630 | Puritans |
| Connecticut | 1636 | |
| Rhode Island | 1647 | |
| New York | 1664 | |
| New Jersey | 1664 | |
| Pennsylvania | 1681 | |
| Delaware | 1638 | |
| Maryland | 1632 | |
| Virginia | 1607 | |
| North Carolina | 1663 | |
| South Carolina | 1712 | |
| Georgia | 1733 | |

# Student Guide
## Lesson 2: Breaks with Tradition: Anne Hutchinson and Mary Dyer

Anne Hutchinson and Mary Dyer were two women who defied Puritan beliefs and practices. Rebels with a cause, they had the courage to face some terrible consequences for what they believed.

## Lesson Objectives

- Describe the status of women in Puritan society.
- Describe the consequences of Anne Hutchinson's break with Puritan tradition.
- Identify Mary Dyer as a Puritan who became a Quaker and was executed for her beliefs.
- Compare and contrast the views of New England dissenters, including Hutchinson and Dyer.

# PREPARE

Approximate lesson time is 60 minutes.

## Materials

For the Student

    💻 Rebels with a Cause

    A History of US (Concise Edition), Volume A (Prehistory to 1800) by Joy Hakim

    History Journal

# LEARN
## Activity 1: Anne Hutchinson and Mary Dyer (Offline)
### Instructions
### Check Your Reading (Chapter 36, pages 168–171)

- Complete the Rebels with a Cause sheet.
- Ask an adult to check your answers.

### Discuss

Discuss with an adult the ways the Puritan view of women and the Quaker view of women differed from each other.

### Read On

Suppose a neighbor for some reason didn't like you and announced to the neighborhood that you were a witch. Would you be thrown in jail or put to death? Probably not, but in 1692 that event did happen in a small village in Massachusetts. In today's reading, you will learn how suspicion and mass hysteria led to the witchcraft trials in Salem.

Read Chapter 37, pages 172–175.

### Vocabulary

You'll see the term "city upon a hill" as you read. Write a brief definition in your History Journal when you come to it.

---

Name _____     Date _____

## Rebels with a Cause

**Three Rebels** Roger Williams, Anne Hutchinson, and Mary Dyer all disagreed with certain Puritan beliefs. But what beliefs did each one hold? What did each one oppose? How did each one stand up for his or her own beliefs? Write the correct name after each of the following descriptions:

1. Believed in freedom of conscience: _____

2. Believed that ordinary people could interpret the Bible: _____

3. Believed in the separation of church and state: _____

4. Refused to swear allegiance to the king: _____

5. Believed that the king had no right to take Indian land: _____

6. Founded the colony that became Rhode Island: _____

7. Was hanged on Boston Common: _____

8. Was killed in New York: _____

9. Wrote a book to teach others the language of the Narraganset Indians: _____

10. Became a Quaker: _____

**Thinking Cap Question!** Anne Hutchinson and Mary Dyer were friends. Write a conversation that they might have had with one another in your History Journal. Make sure that their conversation reflects how they felt about the Puritans.

Adapted from *A History of US*

# Student Guide
## Lesson 3: Visiting Salem

In 1692 trouble started brewing in the Salem area. Neighbors became suspicious of one another and began to accuse each other of being witches. Mass hysteria led to witch trials, hangings, and burnings.

### Lesson Objectives
- Explain the origins and results of the witchcraft trials in Salem.
- Explain the meaning of the phrase "city upon a hill."

---

## PREPARE

Approximate lesson time is 60 minutes.

### Materials

For the Student

   📖 A Visit to Salem

   A History of US (Concise Edition), Volume A (Prehistory to 1800) by Joy Hakim

   History Journal

   paper, construction, 9" x 12"

   pencils, colored, 16 colors or more

---

## LEARN
### Activity 1: Of Witches and Dinosaurs (Offline)
### Instructions
**Check Your Reading (Chapter 37, pages 172–175)**

- Discuss Chapter 37 with an adult.
- Complete the Visit to Salem sheet.
- Ask an adult to check your answers.

**Use What You Know**

Create a Time Line

- Visit the Salem Witch Trials website:
  http://school.discoveryeducation.com/schooladventures/salemwitchtrials/
- Create a time line of the accusations, examinations, trials, and hangings.
- Print images or illustrate the different events on the time line.
- Put the time line in your History Journal.

---

**Read On**

The Puritans were good, strong, intelligent people, even though they made some terrible mistakes. They were independent thinkers, too, and sometimes they disagreed with each other. America was big enough that those who wanted to could move on and start a new settlement. Some people started new settlements for religious reasons. Others did it because they wanted more farmland. Of course, moving to new areas meant pushing into Indian land. Would this cause conflicts between the Indians and the settlers?

Learn how the Connecticut and New Hampshire colonies were founded and how the growth of English settlement led to war.

Read Chapter 38, pages 176–179, and Chapter 39, pages 180–183. As you read the chapters, prepare to discuss the following:

1. How were the people who colonized Maine and New Hampshire different from earlier New England colonists?
2. How did the European idea of land ownership differ from the Indian idea?
3. Why was Connecticut founded?
4. Who were John Mason and Ferdinando Gorges?
5. What caused the Pequot War?
6. What led to King Philip's War, and what was the outcome?

Name _____      Date _____

## A Visit to Salem

Pretend that you are a traveler who is visiting the new colonies in the 1690s. You have just arrived in Salem. Fill in the missing words in your diary.

Dear Diary,

Well, here I am in Salem, in the (1) _____ Colony. Most people here belong to one religious group, and call themselves (2) _____.
They can be very judgmental and self-(3) _____ people who are sure that they and only they know the truth! They read the (4) _____ every day and believe that only a few people are saved by God. Those who are saved are members of God's (5) _____, and must lead very good, religious lives. Those who are not saved will go to a terrible hell filled with fires.

Life was pretty scary here recently. Several young girls were acting very strange. They said that their servant, a poor woman from the West Indies named (6) _____ was a (7) _____, possessed by evil spirits. Many were accused of being possessed and more than one hundred people were put on (8) _____. Altogether (9) _____ people were put to death.

Off to Boston tomorrow. I hope things are a little more peaceful there!

**Thinking Cap Question!** Suppose the traveler were able to interview the judges that presided over the witch trials. Write three interview questions the traveler would ask in your History Journal. Answer them as you think the judges might have answered.

Adapted from *A History of US*

# Student Guide
## Lesson 4: Elsewhere in New England

A growing number of English settlers spread farther onto Indian land. The Indians believed land was to be shared, not owned, but the settlers thought they had taken control from the Indians. Indian resentment of spreading English settlement soon led to war.

### Lesson Objectives

- Demonstrate mastery of important knowledge and skills in previous lessons.
- Chart the founding of Connecticut and New Hampshire.
- Describe the differences in European and Native American attitudes toward land ownership and land use.
- Explain the origins and results of the Pequot War and King Philip's War.
- Explain the reasons for the lack of Indian unity in fighting Europeans.
- Describe the status of women in Puritan society.
- Describe the consequences of Anne Hutchinson's break with Puritan tradition.
- Identify Mary Dyer as a Puritan who became a Quaker and was executed for her beliefs.
- Explain the origins and results of the witchcraft trials in Salem.
- Explain the meaning of the phrase "city upon a hill."
- Identify Roger Williams as the founder of Rhode Island and a supporter of religious toleration and fair treatment of Native Americans.
- Locate the colony of Rhode Island on a map and list its founder, his motives, and his accomplishments.

# PREPARE

Approximate lesson time is 60 minutes.

### Materials

For the Student

- The Pequot War and King Philip's War

A History of US (Concise Edition), Volume A (Prehistory to 1800) by Joy Hakim

History Journal

- Thirteen Colonies, Part 2 Assessment Sheet

# LEARN
## Activity 1: Connecticut, New Hampshire, and Maine (Offline)

### Instructions
**Check Your Reading (Chapter 38, pages 176–179, and Chapter 39, pages 180–183)**
Discuss Chapters 38 and 39 with an adult.

### Use What You Know

- Label New Hampshire and Connecticut on the map on the Thirteen Colonies sheet from the Breaks with Tradition: Roger Williams lesson.
- Complete the sections for New Hampshire and Connecticut on the chart on the same sheet.

- Color the New England colonies green on the map.
- Use the Pequot War and King Philip's War sheet to create a storyboard explaining the causes and results of these two wars. Present the storyboard to an adult. (A storyboard is a tool that filmmakers, multimedia designers, and animators use to visually represent a storyline. A storyboard does not use a lot of detail. Instead, it sketches out the story in a brief, skeleton-like way. One idea is to use a "cartoon" format with characters and speech bubbles.)

**Look Back**

Use the flash cards to review information on New England before you take the mid-unit assessment.

**Read On**

The New England colonies were New Hampshire, Massachusetts, Connecticut, and Rhode Island. These colonies were English colonies. But in the 1600s, Holland and Sweden founded colonies in America, too. Men nicknamed Silvernails and Big Tub were the leaders of New Netherland and New Sweden. Do you know where these colonies were and what they are called today? Here's a clue: In 1664 the English took control of them and renamed New Netherland in honor of the Duke of York.

Read Chapter 40, pages 184–187, and Chapter 41, pages 188–190. Find the answers to the following questions.

1. What role did trading play in both New Netherland and New Sweden?
2. What happened to the Dutch and Swedish colonies in America?
3. How did New Netherland become New York and New Jersey?
4. Give some examples of the ways in which the New Jersey colony was more democratic than many colonies.

Vocabulary

You'll see these words as you read. Write a brief definition for each term as you come to it.

- patroon
- proprietor
- quit rent

---

# ASSESS
## Mid-Unit Assessment: Thirteen Colonies, Part 2 (*Offline*)
You will complete an offline Mid-Unit Assessment covering the main goals for Lessons 1, 2, 3, and 4. lesson. An adult will score the assessment and enter the results online.

---

Name _____     Date _____

## The Pequot War and King Philip's War

Use the boxes to show the causes and results of the wars between settlers and Indians in New England. If you need more boxes, use the back of this sheet.

**The Pequot War**

1.

2.

3.

4.

## King Philip's War

1.

2.

3.

4.

Name _____ Date _____

## Mid-Unit Assessment

This assessment covers Unit 4, Lessons 1–4.

1. Match each term on the left with its description on the right. Write the correct letter on the line in front of the term.

| | |
|---|---|
| _____ Anne Hutchinson | **A.** The founder of Connecticut |
| | **B.** A strong Puritan woman who publicly questioned some of the Puritan ministers' beliefs. She was tried and banished from Massachusetts. |
| _____ Roger Williams | **C.** A martyr who chose to die rather than give up her Quaker beliefs. She was hanged in Boston in 1660. |
| _____ Thomas Hooker | **D.** The founder of Rhode Island. He believed in freedom of conscience and supported fair treatment of Native Americans. |
| _____ Mary Dyer | **E.** The governor of the Massachusetts Bay colony |

2. Which was a result of the Pequot War and King Philip's War?

Ⓐ Very few colonists and Indians died.

Ⓑ Many Indians and colonists died.

Ⓒ Many Indians died, but no colonists were killed.

Ⓓ The Indians were totally wiped out.

3. The idea that the government does not promote or forbid a religion is called _____.

Ⓐ freedom of choice

Ⓑ divine right of kings

Ⓒ freedom of conscience

Ⓓ separation of church and state

**4.** Governor Winthrop called Puritan Massachusetts "a _____," which meant it was a symbol to the rest of the world.

(A) city upon a hill

(B) shining star

(C) land of religious freedom

(D) city with a pure religion

**5.** Among Puritans, women held an equal position to men and were allowed to speak freely in religious meetings.

(A) True

(B) False

**6.** One of the reasons for the lack of Indian unity in fighting Europeans, was that the Indians were descended from different peoples who came in different waves of immigration.

(A) True

(B) False

**7.** Among Quakers, the women could speak as freely as men and were seen as equals in religious meetings.

(A) True

(B) False

**8.** The Salem witch hunts began when a group of girls began accusing people of bewitching them.

(A) True

(B) False

**9.** Describe the difference between European and Native American attitudes toward land use and land ownership.

_____

_____

_____

_____

**10.** Label the following on the map:

- New Hampshire
- Connecticut
- Rhode Island
- Massachusetts

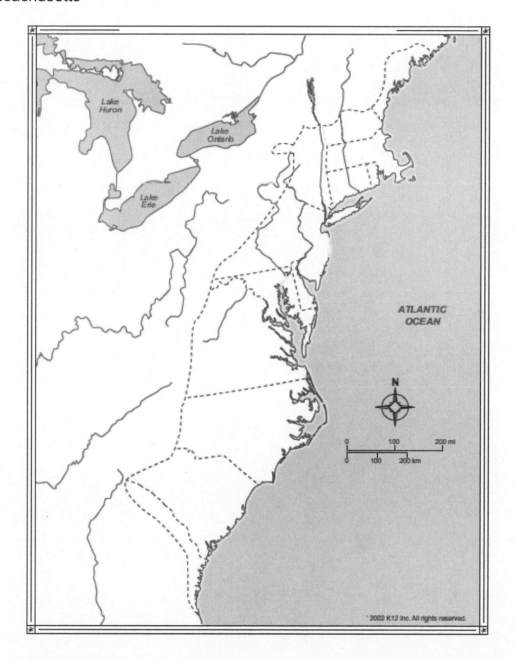

# Student Guide
## Lesson 5: The Middle Colonies

In the 1600s, both Holland and Sweden founded colonies in America. Peter Stuyvesant was the leader of New Netherland, and Johan Printz was the leader of New Sweden. The Duke of York sent a fleet of ships to America to take control of these colonies. Once the English had control, the land was divided and renamed New York and New Jersey.

## Lesson Objectives
- Locate the middle colonies of New York and New Jersey on a map.
- Summarize the transition from New Amsterdam to New York.
- Give examples of the ways in which the New Jersey colony was more democratic than many colonies.
- Complete the chart for New York and New Jersey.

# PREPARE

Approximate lesson time is 60 minutes.

## Materials
  For the Student
   📖 Make the Connection
    A History of US (Concise Edition), Volume A (Prehistory to 1800) by Joy Hakim
    History Journal

# LEARN
## Activity 1: Silvernails and Big Tub, Then West to Jersey *(Offline)*
### Instructions
Check Your Reading (Chapter 40, pages 184–187, and Chapter 41, pages 188–190)

Discuss Chapters 40 and 41 with an adult.

### Use What You Know

- Label New York and New Jersey on the map on the Thirteen Colonies sheet.
- Complete the sections for New York and New Jersey on the chart on the same sheet.
- Complete the Make the Connection sheet.
- Ask an adult to check your answers.

**Read On**

The English colonies of New York and New Jersey were part of the middle colonies. They had representative government and practiced religious freedom. There were other middle colonies as well. They, too, had some form of representation and religious toleration. Which colonies were they? Who were their founders? How much religious toleration was allowed in these colonies?

Read Chapter 44, pages 201–202, and Chapter 42, pages 191–195. Prepare to answer the following questions for discussion.

1.   What was the Calvert family's reason for founding a colony? What was the colony called?
2.   What was the Calverts' attitude toward religious freedom?
3.   Why was England's class system a reason why many came to the New World?
4.   Why did William Penn want a colony?
5.   How was Penn's colony different from most of the other colonies?
6.   How did Delaware become a colony?

Vocabulary

You'll see the term "Toleration Act" as you read. Write a brief definition for this term in your History Journal.

Name _____          Date _____

## Make the Connection

Explain how each pair of names are related to one another. The first pair has been done for you as an example.

1. Henry Hudson/New Netherland

   Henry Hudson was an explorer who claimed land in America for the Netherlands in 1609. The Dutch called the land New Netherland.

2. Dutch West India Company/New Amsterdam

   _____

   _____

   _____

   _____

3. New Netherland/New York

   _____

   _____

   _____

   _____

4. New York/East and West Jersey

   _____

   _____

   _____

   _____

5. East and West Jersey/Jersey

   _____

   _____

   _____

   _____

# Student Guide
## Lesson 6: Toleration Triumphs

The Calvert family founded the Maryland colony as a safe place for Catholics and Protestants to practice religious freedom. William Penn, a Quaker, founded Pennsylvania as a haven for Quakers and people of all religions.

### Lesson Objectives

- Demonstrate mastery of important knowledge and skills in previous lessons.
- Identify Lord Baltimore and the Calverts as the Catholic founders of Maryland as a haven for Catholics.
- Identify William Penn as the Quaker founder of Pennsylvania and the difficulties he and other Quakers faced in England.
- Give examples of toleration and its limits in Pennsylvania and Maryland.
- Chart the founding of Pennsylvania, Delaware, and Maryland.

# PREPARE

Approximate lesson time is 60 minutes.

### Materials

For the Student

     📖 Map of the Thirteen Colonies, 1756

     A History of US (Concise Edition), Volume A (Prehistory to 1800) by Joy Hakim

     History Journal

     📖 Toleration Triumphs Assessment Sheet

# LEARN
## Activity 1: Toleration in Various Forms (Online)

### Instructions

Check Your Reading (Chapter 44, pages 201–202, and Chapter 42, pages 191–195)

- Discuss Chapters 44 and 42 with an adult.
- Label Pennsylvania, Delaware, and Maryland on the map on the Thirteen Colonies sheet.
- Color the middle colonies red.
- Complete the sections for Pennsylvania, Delaware, and Maryland on the chart on the same sheet.

#### Use What You Know

- Decide whether you would rather live in England, Pennsylvania, or Maryland in the 1600s.
- Write a speech explaining your choice and include why you rejected the other two.
- Practice your speech with an adult.

**Look Back**

Use the flash cards to review the middle colonies.

**Read On**

William Penn was a Quaker and the founder of Pennsylvania. Religious freedom, equality for all, and a representative government were just a few of the ideals he used to establish the colony. He also designed the city of Philadelphia. Do you know who Philadelphia's most famous citizen was? He was born in Boston, wrote an almanac, invented many things, signed our Declaration of Independence, and enjoyed flying kites.

Read Chapter 43, pages 196–200. Be prepared to answer the following questions.

1. Name three things Ben Franklin invented.
2. Who was Silence Dogood?
3. Why did Ben Franklin leave Boston and go to Philadelphia?
4. What was *Poor Richard's Almanack?*

---

# ASSESS
## Lesson Assessment: Toleration Triumphs (*Offline*)
You will complete an offline assessment covering the main goals for the lesson. An adult will score the assessment and enter the results online.

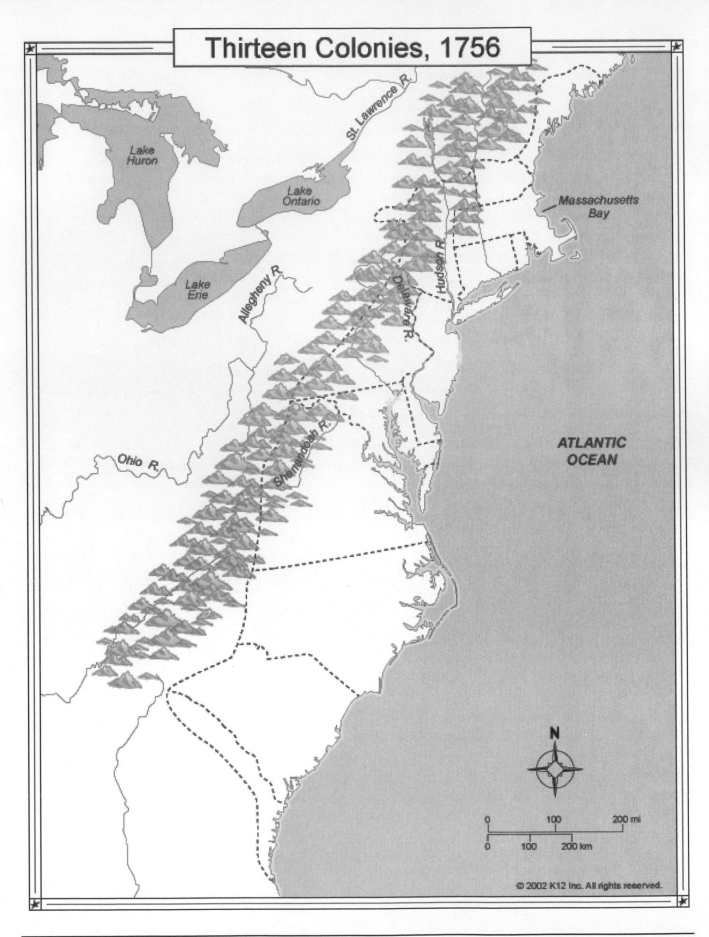

# Thirteen Colonies, 1756

Lake Huron

Lake Ontario

Lake Erie

St. Lawrence R.

Massachusetts Bay

Allegheny R.

Delaware R.

Hudson R.

Ohio R.

Shenandoah R.

ATLANTIC OCEAN

N

| 0 | | 100 | | 200 mi |

| 0 | 100 | 200 km |

Name _____ Date _____

## Lesson Assessment

1. Explain how New Amsterdam became New York.

   _____

   _____

   _____

   _____

2. Name two ways in which the New Jersey colony was more democratic than many colonies.

   _____

   _____

3. Who was the Second Lord Baltimore or Cecil Calvert?

   _____

4. Who was William Penn?

   _____

5. In which middle colony were all religions treated equally? _____

6. In which colony were Catholics and Protestants welcomed, but non-Christians could be executed? _____

Label the following colonies on the map below.

7. Maryland
8. Delaware
9. Pennsylvania
10. New York
11. New Jersey

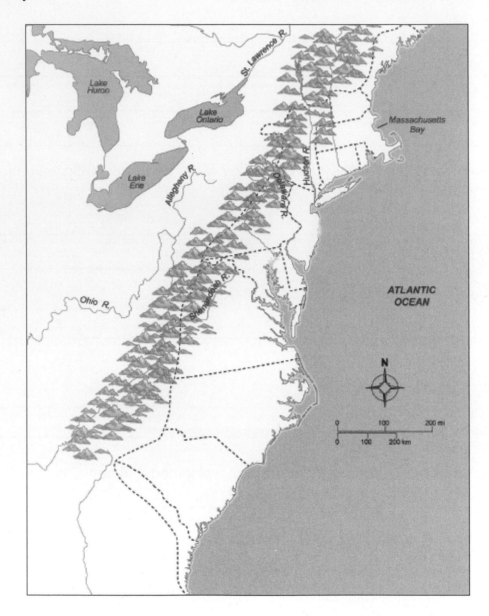

# Student Guide
## Lesson 7: Benjamin Franklin: An American Renaissance Man

Ben Franklin spent most of his life inventing things, including himself. He was a scientist, an inventor, a writer, and a great patriotic American.

### Lesson Objectives
- Read and respond to a brief biography of Benjamin Franklin.
- Analyze Franklin's most important accomplishments.
- Analyze the wisdom of Benjamin Franklin and apply it to today.

# PREPARE

Approximate lesson time is 60 minutes.

### Materials
For the Student

A History of US (Concise Edition), Volume A (Prehistory to 1800) by Joy Hakim

History Journal

# LEARN
## Activity 1: Benjamin Franklin: A Jack-of-All-Trades *(Offline)*
### Instructions
Check Your Reading (Chapter 43, pages 196–200)

Review Chapter 43 using the following questions.

1. Name three things Ben Franklin invented.
2. Who was Silence Dogood?
3. Why did Ben Franklin leave Boston and go to Philadelphia?
4. What was *Poor Richard's Almanack*?

**Use What You Know**

Go online and visit the following website: *Benjamin Franklin: Glimpses of the Man.* Research one of Benjamin Franklin's many accomplishments. Then write one or more paragraphs on the accomplishment and how it has improved the United States. You may use one of the following suggestions or choose your own topic.

- Franklin's success as a printer and author (*Poor Richard's Almanack*)
- His success as a public servant (fire department, public library, hospital)
- His role as an inventor and scientist (electricity, lightning rod, bifocals, Franklin stove)
- His role in politics (coauthor of the Declaration of Independence, diplomat during the American Revolution)

**Read On**

As the people of the middle colonies took control of more land, they changed it in any way they saw fit. They also changed the cultures they brought with them from Europe by allowing greater religious freedom and more representative government. The southern colonies were quite different from the New England and middle colonies. Find out what English traditions the leaders in the South kept. Explore the different pieces of the southern class system. Why was slavery so much more important in the South than in the other colonies as time went on?

Read Chapter 45, pages 203–207, and Chapter 46, pages 208–212.

# *Student Guide*
## Lesson 8: Colonization Heads South

A large plantation was like a small village. The land and workers provided everything, including housing, food, clothing, education, work, and entertainment for the owner and his family. Life for southern tradesmen, small farmers, and slaves was very different from the life of the rich plantation owners. The rich ruling class made strict laws and enjoyed far more privileges than other people in the South.

### Lesson Objectives
- Locate on a map the southern colonies of Virginia, North Carolina, South Carolina, and Georgia.
- Describe plantation life for owners, women, slaves, and small farmers.

# PREPARE

Approximate lesson time is 60 minutes.

### Materials
For the Student

    📖 Living the Good Life

    A History of US (Concise Edition), Volume A (Prehistory to 1800) by Joy Hakim

    History Journal

# LEARN
## Activity 1: Life in the South *(Offline)*
### Instructions
**Check Your Reading (Chapter 45, pages 203–207, and Chapter 46, pages 208–212)**

- Complete the Living the Good Life sheet.
- Discuss your answers with an adult.

### Read On
*This reading prepares you for the next lesson, which is an OPTIONAL lesson.*
In the South, the wealthy class made the laws for the small farmers, skilled workers, and slaves. Do you remember the House of Burgesses in Virginia? It met in the state's capital, Williamsburg. Some of these lawmakers would one day be founders of the United States.

Read Chapter 47, pages 213–216.

Name _____     Date _____

## Living the Good Life

**What If?** What if you had lived in Virginia in the early 1700s? What would your life have been like? Pretend that you are each of the people below. Answer the questions about your life.

### A Plantation Owner's Daughter

1. What does your plantation look like? List five buildings on your plantation: _____

   _____

   _____

2. Do you think your father is like a business executive? How? _____

   _____

   _____

3. There is a party tonight. What are you going to wear? What will your brother wear?

   _____

   _____

4. Did you go to school today? Where? What did you study? _____

   _____

   _____

### A Young Indentured Servant in Williamsburg

5. You work for a silversmith. List three things you did in the shop today. _____

   _____

   _____

6. Are you free to change jobs? Why or why not? _____

   _____

   _____

Adapted from *A History of US*

## A Child of a Virginia Farmer

7. Describe the house you live in. _____

_____

_____

8. Are there any laws about religion? What are they? How do your parents feel about these

    laws? _____

_____

_____

9. How much schooling do you have? What might you do at the age of 15?

_____

_____

## An Eleven-Year-Old Slave Girl

10. You share two houses with other slaves. Describe your living conditions, such as

    housing and food. _____

_____

_____

11. What type of schooling do you have? _____

_____

_____

# Student Guide
## Lesson 9: (Optional) A Visit to Williamsburg

Williamsburg was the capital of Virginia. The members of the House of Burgesses held their meetings in Williamsburg. Several members of the House of Burgesses would one day be the founders of the United States.

Even though you may skip this lesson, you must complete the **Read On** activity before moving on to the next lesson.

### Lesson Objectives
- Use the Internet to acquire information on Williamsburg.
- Describe Williamsburg in colonial times.

# PREPARE

Approximate lesson time is 60 minutes.

### Materials
For the Student

A History of US (Concise Edition), Volume A (Prehistory to 1800) by Joy Hakim

History Journal

# LEARN
## Activity 1. Optional: A Visit to Williamsburg *(Offline)*
### Instructions
**Use What You Know**

Take a virtual field trip to Williamsburg using the following website: *Colonial Williamsburg History*. Explore the following sections:

- Meet the People
- See the Places
- Experience the Life
- Clothing

After exploring the website, complete the following sentence in your History Journal: I would / would not (choose one) have enjoyed living in Colonial Williamsburg because _____.

**Read On**

In Virginia, many of the wealthy colonists kept the customs and traditions of England. The wealthy also made the laws that governed the small farmers, tradesmen, and slaves. Tobacco was the major cash crop. In this activity, you will read about life in the Carolinas.

Read Chapter 48, pages 217–221, and Chapter 49, pages 222–227.

Vocabulary

You'll see these terms as you read. Write a brief definition for each term as you come to it.

- indigo
- Gullah

# Student Guide
## Lesson 10: Colonial Life in the South

South Carolina was a prosperous colony. Its economy was based on rice and indigo. Slave labor was used to grow these cash crops. The upper class was in control of both the economy and the government. North Carolina was different. The colony consisted of free-spirited farmers, religious rebels, and pirates. The last of the 13 colonies to be formed was Georgia. James Oglethorpe was the founder. He wanted a haven for debtors who were jailed in England because they could not pay their debts.

### Lesson Objectives

- Demonstrate mastery of important knowledge and skills taught in previous lessons.
- Identify Charleston on a map and describe the social structure there in colonial times as a mixture of aristocracy, poor whites, and slaves.
- Give examples of democratic practices in North Carolina, including religious toleration.
- Identify James Oglethorpe as the founder of Georgia as a haven for debtors.
- Chart the founding of North Carolina, South Carolina, and Georgia.
- Locate on a map the southern colonies of Virginia, North Carolina, South Carolina, and Georgia.
- Identify Gullah as the language developed by African Americans in South Carolina.

---

# PREPARE

Approximate lesson time is 60 minutes.

### Materials

For the Student

📖 The Carolinas

A History of US (Concise Edition), Volume A (Prehistory to 1800) by Joy Hakim

History Journal

📖 Colonial Life in the South Assessment Sheet

---

# LEARN
## Activity 1: The Final Three Southern Colonies (Offline)

### Instructions

**Check Your Reading (Chapter 48, pages 217–221, and Chapter 49, pages 222–227)**

Complete the Carolinas sheet to check what you learned in Chapter 48. Have an adult check your answers.

Discuss the following questions to review Chapter 49:

1. What was James Oglethorpe's motive for founding Georgia?
2. What did James Oglethorpe want the people to do? What were some of the laws Oglethorpe wanted passed?
3. What were some of the reasons why Oglethorpe's plans didn't work?

---

**Use What You Know**

- Label North Carolina, South Carolina, Georgia, and Charleston on the map on the Thirteen Colonies sheet.
- Color the southern colonies blue.
- Complete the sections for North Carolina, South Carolina, and Georgia on the chart on the same sheet.

**Look Back**

It's time for a review on the southern colonies—use the flash cards. When you've finished, click Student Activity to visit a typical plantation.

---

# ASSESS
## Lesson Assessment: Colonial Life in the South (*Offline*)

You will complete an offline assessment covering the main goals for the lesson. An adult will score the assessment and enter the results online.

Name _____          Date _____

# The Carolinas

North and South Carolina may be neighbors, but they made for very different colonies. Fill in North or South to identify the correct colony. Supply any other missing words to complete each sentence.

1. Named for the English king, _____ Town (Charleston) was the capital of _____ Carolina.

2. Many leaders in _____ Carolina came from the Caribbean island of _____ .

3. As a place where people left one another alone, _____ Carolina may have been the most _____ of all of the colonies.

4. _____ Carolina was a very _____ colony, where a few wealthy people held most of the power.

5. The famous pirate _____ operated off the coast of _____ Carolina.

6. In 1677, some people in _____ Carolina refused to pay _____ to England.

7. Africans probably taught the people in _____ Carolina how to grow _____ , the crop that made slavery profitable there.

8. Unlike other Southern colonies, _____ Carolina had a great city, _____ .

9. Colonists in _____ Carolina tried to set up their own _____ to be free of England.

10. _____ is a language developed by African Americans in _____ Carolina.

**Thinking Cap Question!** Would you rather have lived in North or South Carolina in colonial times? Explain your answer.

Name _____     Date _____

## Lesson Assessment

For questions 1–4, fill in the blanks using the words from the word bank.

| Word Bank | | | | |
| --- | --- | --- | --- | --- |
| aristocratic | Charleston | Williamsburg | Gullah | rice |
| tobacco | James Oglethorpe | Blackbeard | indigo | |

1. The founder of Georgia, _____, wanted to provide a haven for debtors.

2. The language developed by African Americans in South Carolina is called

   _____ .

3. _____ was the major cash crop in South Carolina that made slavery very profitable.

4. _____ was a famous pirate who operated off the coast of North Carolina.

5. Give two examples of how North Carolina may have been the most democratic of all the colonies.

   _____

   _____

   _____

   _____

**6.** Label the following on the map of the thirteen colonies:

- Virginia
- North Carolina
- South Caroline
- Georgia
- Charleston

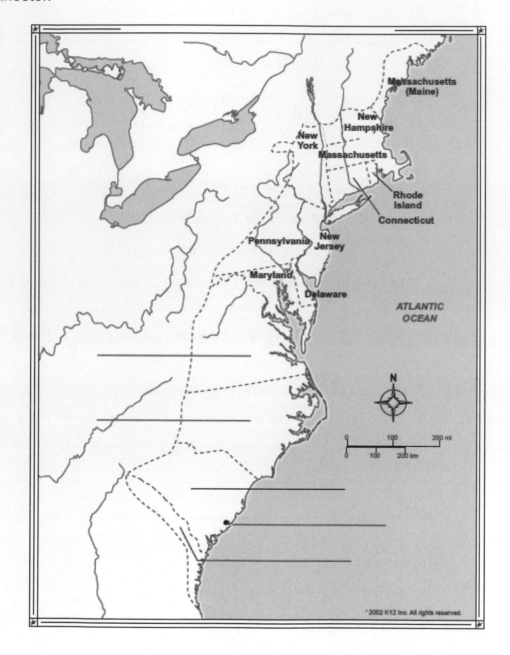

# Student Guide
## Lesson 11: Triangles of Trade

New England shipping developed triangular trade routes. These routes linked New England with England, Africa, the West Indies, and America's Atlantic ports. Some of the trade items included forest products, rice, indigo, furs, and tobacco. Slaves were also traded and transported from Africa to the West Indies and America.

### Lesson Objectives
- Analyze a map of colonial trade and trace the major routes and products of the triangular trade.
- Summarize information gained from the diary of Olaudah.
- Categorize resources as fossil fuels or animal, plant, or mineral resources.
- Categorize resources as renewable or nonrenewable.
- Interpret maps for information about natural resources.

# PREPARE

Approximate lesson time is 60 minutes.

### Materials

For the Student

    📖 Map of Triangle Trade

    📖 Triangular Journeys

    A History of US (Concise Edition), Volume A (Prehistory to 1800) by Joy Hakim

    Understanding Geography: Map Skills and Our World (Level 5)

    History Journal

# LEARN
## Activity 1: Triangular Journeys *(Offline)*
### Instructions
### Read

Read Chapter 50, pages 228–234.

### Check Your Reading (Chapter 50, pages 228–234)

Complete the Triangular Journeys sheet. You may use the map of Triangle Trade as a reference. Have an adult check your answers.

### Use What You Know

- In your History Journal, list some things you learned about Olaudah by reading the excerpts from Olaudah's diary.
- Read your list to an adult. Point out information from the excerpts that support your list.

### Resources and Trade

In colonial times, colonists got many things they needed from their own community. Most people grew their own food, made their own clothes, and even built their own furniture. They also brought in some manufactured products from Great Britain. Maps can help you learn more about an area's economy.

- Read Activity 7, "Resources and Trade" (pages 28–31), in *Understanding Geography*.
- Answer Questions 1–13 in your History Journal.
- If you have time, you may want to answer the Skill Builder Questions on page 31.
- After you have finished you should compare your answers with the ones in the Teacher Guide.

# ASSESS

## Lesson Assessment: Triangles of Trade (*Online*)

Answer the online geography questions for this assessment covering the main goals of this lesson. Your assessment will be scored by the computer.

Name _____     Date _____

# Triangular Journeys

Suppose that you are traveling by ship in the year 1700. Answer these questions about the stops on your journey from Massachusetts to the West Indies:

## New England

1. You left your family's farm in Massachusetts because you couldn't make a living. Why was it so hard to farm in New England? _____

   _____

2. Was it hard to find a job in industry? Why? _____

   _____

   _____

3. How did codfish influence Yankee trade? _____

   _____

   _____

## England

4. Your ship is part of the Triangular Trade. Why has it come to England? _____

   _____

5. Name two products your ship has brought to England. _____

   _____

## Africa

6. What cargo does your ship carry from England to Africa? Why? _____

   _____

   _____

7. What cargo does your ship carry from Africa to the West Indies? Why? _____

   _____

   _____

**West Indies**

8. What is the African cargo traded for in the West Indies? _____

_____

9. What is the West Indian cargo used for in New England? _____

_____

Adapted from *A History of US*

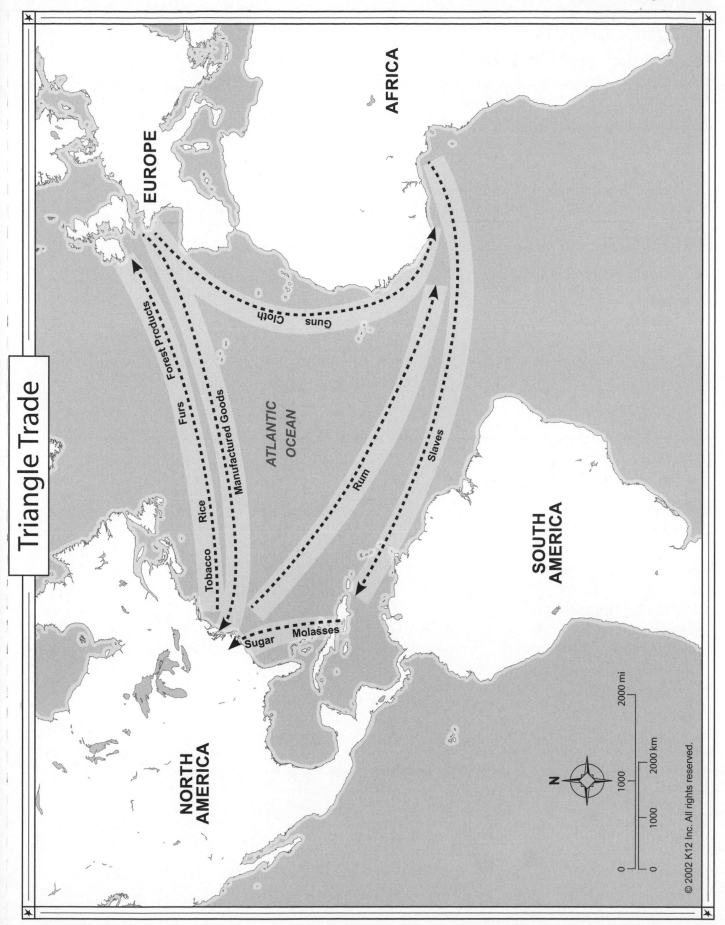

Triangle Trade

# Student Guide
## Lesson 12: Unit Review

You've completed Unit 4, Thirteen Colonies, Part 2. It's time to review what you've learned. You'll take the Unit Assessment in the next lesson.

(This review might refer to topics presented in optional lessons in this unit.)

### Lesson Objectives
- Demonstrate mastery of important knowledge and skills taught in previous lessons.

# PREPARE

Approximate lesson time is 60 minutes.

### Materials
For the Student

      📠 Thirteen Colonies, 1756

      📠 Triangles of Trade

      A History of US (Concise Edition), Volume A (Prehistory to 1800) by Joy Hakim

      History Journal

# LEARN
## Activity 1: A Look Back (Offline)
### Instructions
#### Online Review

Use the following to review this unit:

- The Big Picture
- Flash Cards
- Time Line
- Thirteen Colonies, 1756 map
- Triangle Trade map

#### History Journal Review

Now go offline and review more by going through your History Journal. Look at the sheets you completed for this unit. Review your vocabulary words. If you completed any writing assignments, read them. Take your time. Your History Journal is a great resource for a unit review.

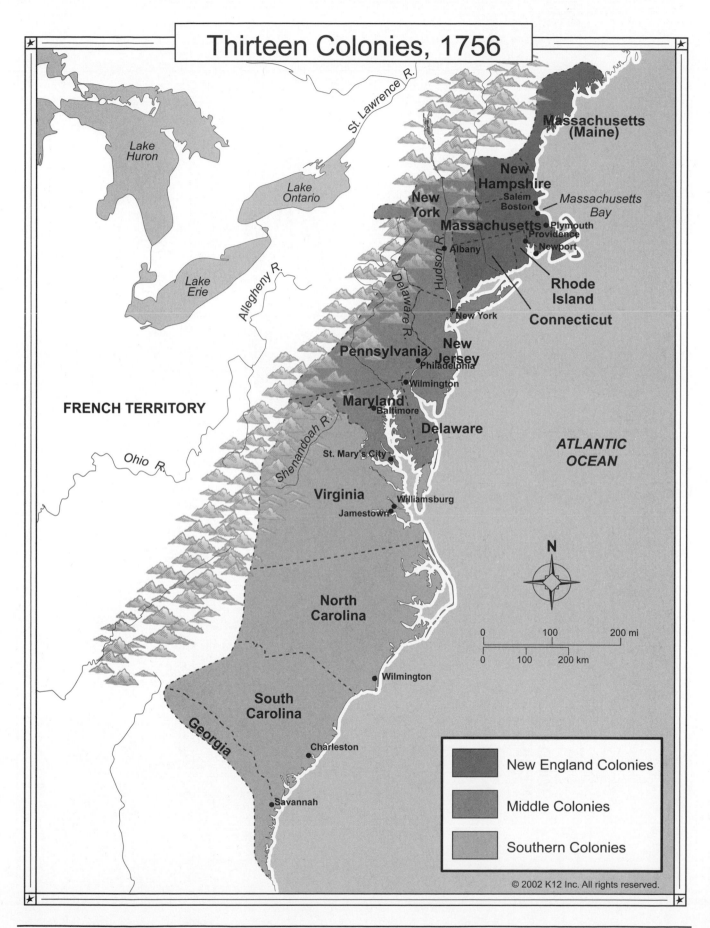

# Thirteen Colonies, 1756

Lake Huron

Lake Ontario

Lake Erie

St. Lawrence R.

Allegheny R.

Ohio R.

**FRENCH TERRITORY**

Shenandoah R.

Delaware R.

Hudson R.

Massachusetts (Maine)

New Hampshire

New York

Salem
Boston
*Massachusetts Bay*

Massachusetts

Albany

Plymouth
Providence
Newport

**Rhode Island**

**Connecticut**

New York

**Pennsylvania**

New Jersey

Philadelphia

Wilmington

Maryland
Baltimore

**Delaware**

St. Mary's City

Virginia

Williamsburg
Jamestown

North Carolina

Wilmington

South Carolina

Georgia

Charleston

Savannah

*ATLANTIC OCEAN*

N

0    100    200 mi
0    100    200 km

New England Colonies

Middle Colonies

Southern Colonies

© 2002 K12 Inc. All rights reserved.

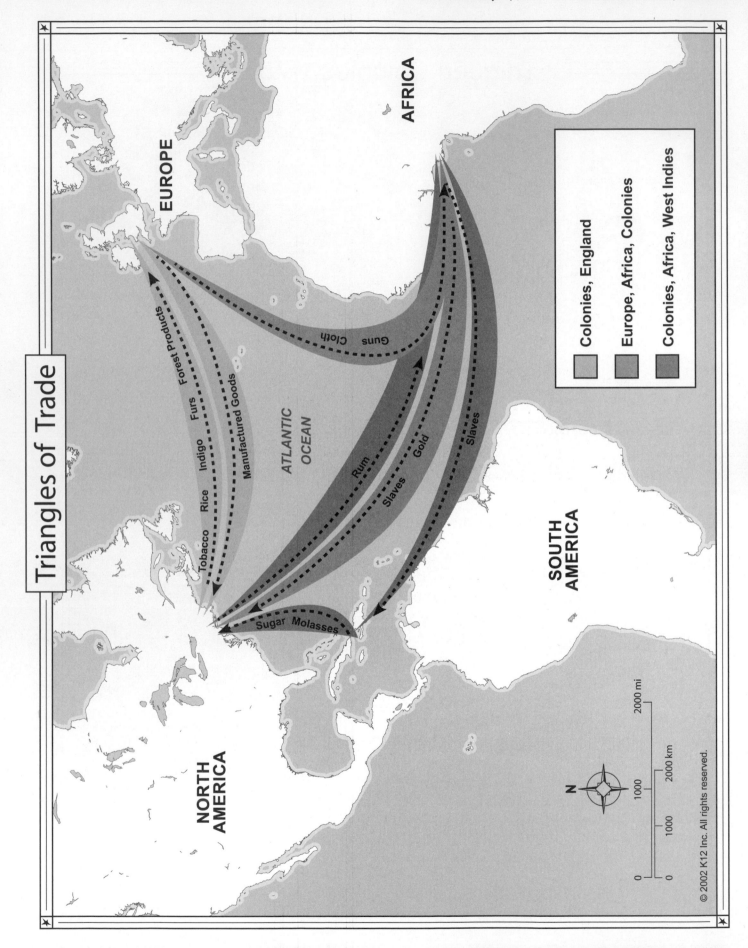

Triangles of Trade

EUROPE

AFRICA

NORTH AMERICA

SOUTH AMERICA

ATLANTIC OCEAN

Forest Products

Furs

Manufactured Goods

Indigo

Rice

Tobacco

Cloth   Guns

Rum

Slaves

Gold

Slaves

Sugar   Molasses

Colonies, England

Europe, Africa, Colonies

Colonies, Africa, West Indies

N

2000 mi

2000 km

1000

1000

0

0

© 2002 K12 Inc. All rights reserved.

# Student Guide
## Lesson 13: Unit Assessment

You've finished this unit on the 13 colonies. Now take the Unit Assessment, and then read today's assignment.

### Lesson Objectives

- Analyze the geography of the eastern seaboard of the United States.
- Describe the status of women in Puritan society.
- Describe the consequences of Anne Hutchinson's break with Puritan tradition.
- Explain the origins and results of the witchcraft trials in Salem.
- Chart the founding of Connecticut and New Hampshire.
- Explain the origins and results of the Pequot War and King Philip's War.
- Locate the middle colonies of New York and New Jersey on a map.
- Complete the chart for New York and New Jersey.
- Identify Lord Baltimore and the Calverts as the Catholic founders of Maryland as a haven for Catholics.
- Identify William Penn as the Quaker founder of Pennsylvania and the difficulties he and other Quakers faced in England.
- Chart the founding of Pennsylvania, Delaware, and Maryland.
- Analyze Franklin's most important accomplishments.
- Locate on a map the southern colonies of Virginia, North Carolina, South Carolina, and Georgia.
- Identify James Oglethorpe as the founder of Georgia as a haven for debtors.
- Identify Roger Williams as the founder of Rhode Island and a supporter of religious toleration and fair treatment of Native Americans.
- Locate the colony of Rhode Island on a map and list its founder, his motives, and his accomplishments.

# PREPARE

Approximate lesson time is 60 minutes.

## Materials

For the Student

🖵 Thirteen Colonies, Part 2 Assessment Sheet

A History of US (Concise Edition), Volume A (Prehistory to 1800) by Joy Hakim

History Journal

# ASSESS

## Unit Assessment: Thirteen Colonies, Part 2 (*Offline*)

Complete the offline Unit Assessment. Your Learning Coach will score it and enter the results online.

# LEARN
## Activity 1: Chapter 51 *(Offline)*
### Instructions
### Read On

*The assigned reading prepares you for the next lesson, which is an OPTIONAL lesson.*

Peter Zenger founded a newspaper called the *New York Weekly Journal*. He used the newspaper to criticize the New York governor and his politics. The governor had Zenger arrested and tried. Who was Zenger's attorney? What was the outcome of the trial? How does the Zenger trial affect life in the United States today?

Read Chapter 51, pages 236–239.

Name _____ Date _____

# Unit Assessment

1. Match each term on the left with its description on the right. Write the correct letter on the line in front of the term.

_____ James Oglethorpe

**A.** Founder of Rhode Island; believed in freedom of conscience and supported fair treatment of Native Americans

_____ Cecil Calvert

**B.** Judge who sentenced several witches to death; later apologized

_____ Benjamin Franklin

**C.** Strong Puritan who publicly questioned some of the Puritan ministers' beliefs; was tried and banished from Massachusetts

_____ Thomas Hooker

**D.** The second Lord Baltimore and founder of Maryland

_____ Anne Hutchinson

**E.** Founder of Georgia; wanted to provide a haven for debtors

**F.** Founder of Connecticut

_____ William Penn

**G.** Quaker founder of Pennsylvania

**H.** Inventor of bifocal glasses, the lightning rod, the one-arm desk chair, an efficient stove, and daylight saving time

_____ Roger Williams

Fill in the blanks using the following terms.

| | | | | |
|---|---|---|---|---|
| Blackbeard | Charleston | Williamsburg | Quakers | Puritans |
| land | Providence | Salem | Gullah | religion | New York |

2. _____ was the major cause of King Philip's War and the Pequot War.

3. A group of girls accused a servant and neighbors of witchcraft. The result was the witch hunt hysteria in the town of _____ and the deaths of 20 people.

4. During colonial times, the society in _____, South Carolina, was a mixture of aristocracy, poor whites, and slaves.

5. Among _____, women could speak as freely as men and were seen as equals in religious meetings. Among _____, women held a secondary position to men and were expected to be quiet.

6. Roger Williams chose the location of _____ as the capital of Rhode Island because of its good natural harbor.

7. The Dutch colony of New Netherland became the British colony of _____.

8. You live in a small wooden house with one big room and a sleeping loft. The only clothes you have are those you wear, and a Sunday shirt. You probably had a year of schooling and know how to read. Who are you?

   Ⓐ an indentured servant

   Ⓑ a child of a plantation owner

   Ⓒ a child of a small farmer

   Ⓓ a slave

9. You live near the tobacco fields on a large plantation. You can't read and never will be taught how. You are someone's property. Who are you?

   Ⓐ an indentured servant

   Ⓑ a child of a plantation owner

   Ⓒ a child of a small farmer

   Ⓓ a slave

10. You live with your family in a great house with many rooms and many servants. You wear fancy clothes when visitors come to stay for a party. Who are you?

    Ⓐ an indentured servant

    Ⓑ a child of a plantation owner

    Ⓒ a child of a small farmer

    Ⓓ a slave

11. Most Europeans believed the individuals could own land and use it as they saw fit. Most Indians believed that the land belonged to God and tribes as a whole shared in the use of it.

(A) True

(B) False

12. Maryland passed a Toleration Act that allowed for freedom of religion for all Christians, Jews and atheists.

(A) True

(B) False

13. Slaves were brought from Africa to the Americas as part of a triangle of trade in colonial times.

(A) True

(B) False

**14.** Label the following on the map of the thirteen colonies.

| | | |
|---|---|---|
| New Jersey | Delaware | Maryland |
| Massachusetts | South Carolina | Pennsylvania |
| Virginia | Rhode Island | Connecticut |
| New York | Georgia | |
| North Carolina | New Hampshire | |

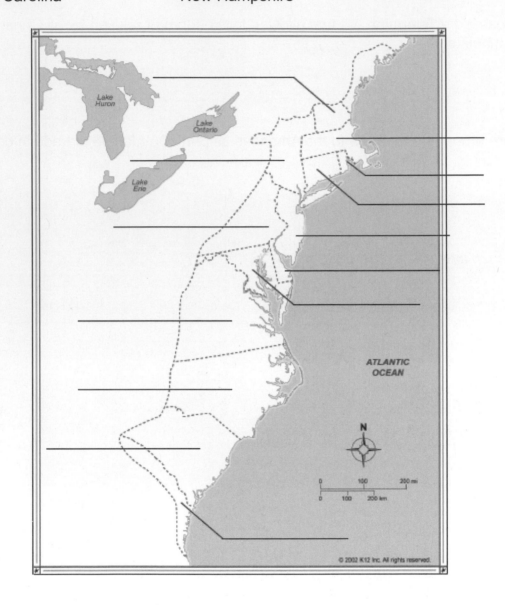

# Student Guide
## Lesson 1: (Optional) Peter's Press

John Adams said that the real American Revolution took place in the "minds and hearts of the people." Those people began as loyal and proud citizens of the most powerful and democratic nation in the world—"Great Britain. They ended by taking up arms against the king. Their journey toward independence started years before any shots were fired.

The trial of John Peter Zenger may seem unimportant today. But Zenger, his lawyer, and the people of New York did something very good for all of us. They defended their rights to freedom of the press and trial by jury. Those are rights we have today. And the trial helped bring the colonies together.

Even though you may skip this lesson, you must complete the **Read On** activity before moving on to the next lesson.

### Lesson Objectives
- Identify Peter Zenger.
- Define *libel.*
- Summarize the importance of the Peter Zenger Trial

# PREPARE

Approximate lesson time is 60 minutes.

### Materials
For the Student

    📖 Hamilton Said It First!

    A History of US (Concise Edition), Volume A (Prehistory to 1800) by Joy Hakim

    History Journal

# LEARN
## Activity 1. Optional: Freedom of the Press *(Offline)*
### Instructions
**Check Your Reading (Chapter 51, pages 236–239)**

Go over what you learned in Chapter 51 using the Hamilton Said It First! sheet.

**Read On**

The French and Indian War changed the future of the North American continent. Do you know who were allies and who were enemies in that war? Did you know that George Washington was a soldier in the British army during that war? He and others learned valuable lessons that helped them shake off British rule over 20 years later. How did that happen? And why?

Read Chapter 52, pages 240–245, and Chapter 53, pages 246–251.

Vocabulary

You'll see these terms as you read. Write a brief definition for each term in your History Journal.

- frontier
- Huguenot
- surveyor
- lay siege

Name _____    Date _____

## Hamilton Said It First!

At Peter Zenger's trial, Andrew Hamilton said:

> *"Free men have the right to oppose arbitrary power by speaking and writing truths… to assert with courage the sense they have of the blessings of liberty, the value they put upon it, and their resolution… to prove it one of the greatest blessings heaven can bestow… There is no libel if the truth is told."*

In questions 1–4, your mission is to locate the word or words from Hamilton's quote that best fit in the blanks.

1.  In his newspaper, Peter Zenger published articles criticizing the Governor's use of

    _____ _____."

2.  Because it was against the law to criticize the king or his appointees, the Attorney

    General accused Peter Zenger of committing "_____."

3.  Hamilton believed Zenger was not guilty of this charge because in Zenger's newspaper

    articles the "_____ _____ _____."

4.  Hamilton felt that more than just Peter Zenger was on trial. He felt that the larger concept

    of American "_____" was at stake.

5.  Gouverneur Morris, one of the writers of the Constitution, said: "The trial of Zenger in 1735 was the germ of American freedom, the morning star of that liberty which subsequently revolutionized America." What did Hamilton and Morris agree about?

    _____

    _____

    _____

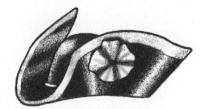

**Thinking Cap Question!** Do you think that television and newspaper reporters should be free to criticize the president as much as they like? Why or why not? Write your answer in your History Journal.

Adapted from *A History of US*

# Student Guide
## Lesson 2: The French and Indian War

The French and Indian War changed the future of the North American continent. It also taught colonial leaders, such as George Washington, valuable lessons that would later help them against the British. With help from their colonial and Native American allies, the British won the war. But another conflict soon began—this time over who would pay for the war.

## Lesson Objectives
- Analyze Franklin's "Join or Die" to gain understanding of political cartoons.
- Explain the causes of the French and Indian War as competition between France and England for land and power.
- Identify George Washington as a soldier in the British Army during the French and Indian War.

# PREPARE

Approximate lesson time is 60 minutes.

## Materials

For the Student

    📖 Understanding Political Cartoons

    A History of US (Concise Edition), Volume A (Prehistory to 1800) by Joy Hakim

    History Journal

# LEARN
## Activity 1: British Victory (Offline)

### Instructions

**Check Your Reading (Chapter 52, pages 240–245, and Chapter 53, pages 246–251)**

Review Chapters 52 and 53 by discussing the following questions with an adult:

1. What was the major cause of the French and Indian War?
2. What lessons did George Washington learn from the French and Indian War?
3. How did the British expect to pay for the high cost of the war?
4. Look at the map on page 249. What do the locations of the forts have in common? Why do you think that is?

## Use What You Know

Diary Entry

It's time for battle! You're part of the Virginia militia that served with George Washington in the Ohio River Valley. In your History Journal, write a diary entry that describes how you planned to drive the French out of Fort Duquesne. Describe what happened during your campaign to rid the frontier and Fort Duquesne of the French. Did it all go as planned?

Document Analysis

Discuss Franklin's "Join or Die" political cartoon with an adult. Then complete the Understanding Political Cartoons sheet.

## Read On

Learn what Great Britain got as a result of winning the war. What do you think Britain's Indian allies, the Iroquois, got for helping the British? And who do you think wanted to move into all that land west of the Appalachians?

Read Chapter 54, pages 252–257. As you read, keep these questions in mind:

- Did the British encourage the colonists to take land west of the Appalachians?
- What did the colonists think of the British proclamation?

Vocabulary

You'll see these terms as you read. Write a brief definition for each in your History Journal.

- mission
- speculator
- pioneer

Name _____     Date _____

## Understanding Political Cartoons

Benjamin Franklin, 1754

Answer the following questions after studying Benjamin Franklin's cartoon.

1. What is the title of the cartoon? _____

2. What does each segment of the serpent represent? _____

_____

3. The section of the snake nearest the head is labeled "N.E." for New England (New Hampshire, Massachusetts, Rhode Island, and Connecticut). Travel south from there to the snake's tail and list the colonies represented in the cartoon.

_____

_____

_____

4. Which of the 13 colonies are not represented? _____

5. Explain the message of Benjamin Franklin's cartoon. _____

_____

6. How many years passed between the time Franklin drew this cartoon and the start of the Revolutionary War? _____

# Student Guide
## Lesson 3: Looking West

After the French and Indian War, British colonists expected to settle west of the Appalachians. Native Americans knew this would mean the end of their lands. The British tried to stop the migration of colonists with the Proclamation of 1763, which said that no colonists could settle west of the Appalachian Mountains. But the pioneer spirit was too strong.

## Lesson Objectives

- Summarize the outcome of the French and Indian War as the end of the French presence in most of North America.
- Describe the problems faced by Native Americans in the Ohio River Valley after 1763, including encroachment by white settlers.
- Describe the problems the British government faced after 1763 in trying to limit westward migration and why many Americans wanted to go west.
- Locate the Appalachian Mountains on a map and explain that the British did not want migration across them for reasons of economics and security.

---

# PREPARE

Approximate lesson time is 60 minutes.

## Materials

For the Student

- Map of Land Claims in the New World, 1750
- Map of Land Claims in the New World, 1763
- Talking Heads: Proclamation of 1763
- The French and Indian War: Before and After

  A History of US (Concise Edition), Volume A (Prehistory to 1800) by Joy Hakim

  History Journal

---

# LEARN
## Activity 1: Heading West? *(Offline)*
### Instructions
**Check Your Reading (Chapter 54, pages 252–257)**

Go over Chapter 54 by discuss the following questions with an adult.

1. Did Native Americans benefit from the French and Indian war?
2. Why did England forbid settlement west of the Appalachian Mountains?
3. How did colonists respond to the Proclamation of 1763? Why?
4. How do you think Native Americans might have viewed the Proclamation of 1763? Why?
5. What routes did pioneers travel to reach the West?
6. Who was Daniel Boone?

---

**Use What You Know**

French and Indian War: Before and After

Use the maps provided to complete the French and Indian War: Before and After sheet. Check your work with an adult.

Talking Heads: Proclamation of 1763

Review the Proclamation of 1763 by completing the Talking Heads: Proclamation of 1763 sheet. Check your answers with an adult.

Name _____          Date _____

# The French and Indian War: Before and After

Color the land the British controlled before the French and Indian War in red. Color the land the French controlled in yellow. Label the English colonies, Mexico, Florida, Newfoundland, Boston, Montreal, Great Lakes, Mississippi River, Ohio River, and Fort Duquesne.

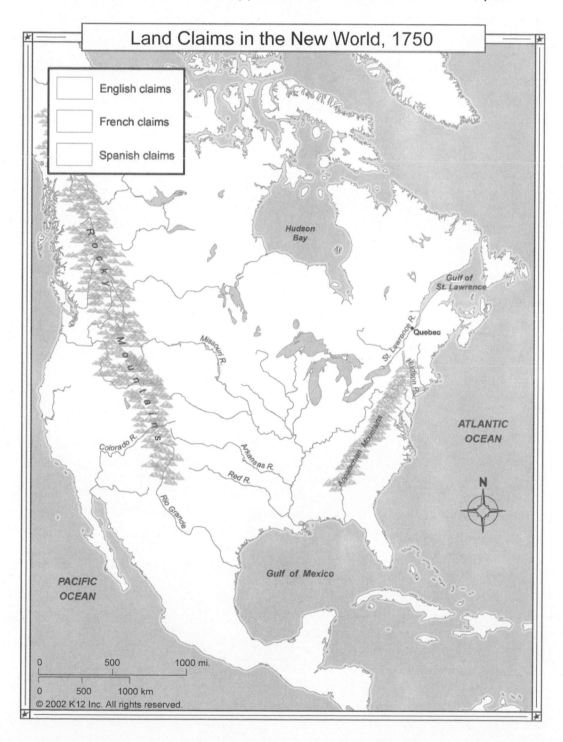

Land Claims in the New World, 1750

English claims

French claims

Spanish claims

Color the land the British controlled after the French and Indian War in red. Color the land the French controlled in yellow. Label the English colonies, Mexico, Florida, Newfoundland, Boston, Montreal, Great Lakes, Mississippi River, Ohio River, and Fort Duquesne.

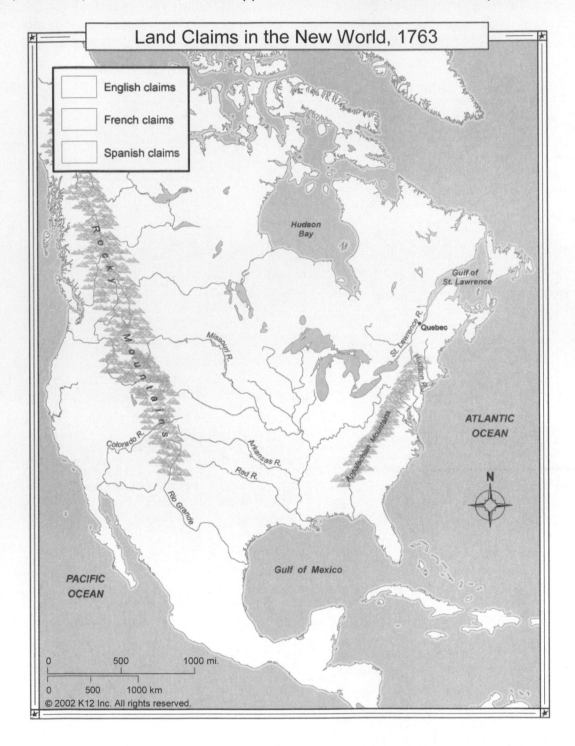

Land Claims in the New World, 1763

English claims

French claims

Spanish claims

# Land Claims in the New World, 1763

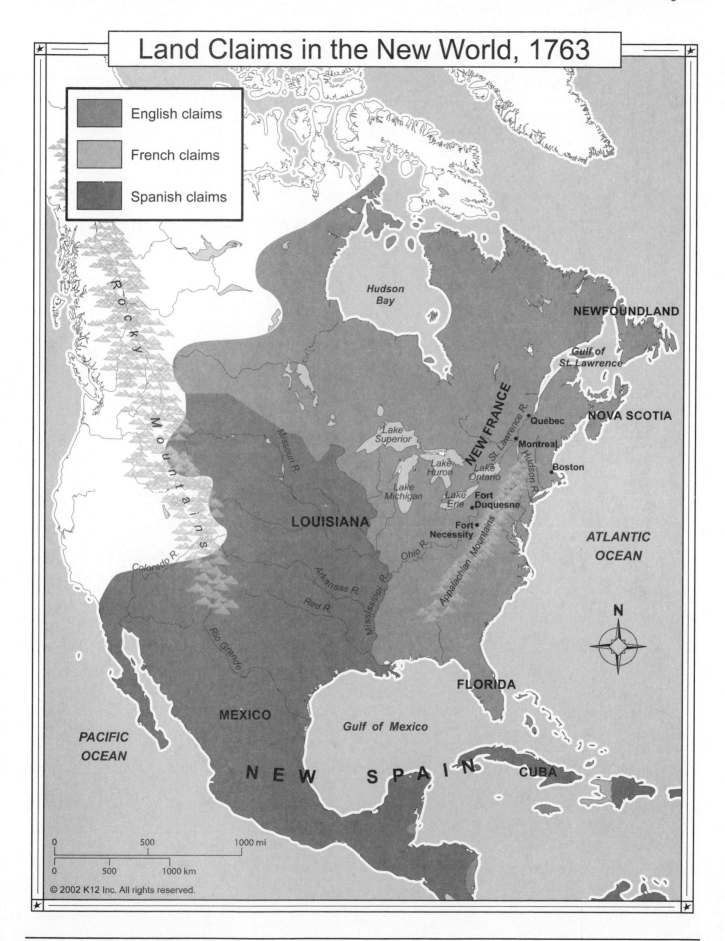

English claims
French claims
Spanish claims

PACIFIC OCEAN

ROCKY Mountains

Hudson Bay

NEWFOUNDLAND

Gulf of St. Lawrence

NOVA SCOTIA

NEW FRANCE

Quebec

Montreal

Boston

Lake Superior

Lake Huron

Lake Michigan

Lake Ontario

St. Lawrence R.

Hudson R.

Missouri R.

LOUISIANA

Lake Erie

Fort Duquesne

Fort Necessity

Ohio R.

Appalachian Mountains

ATLANTIC OCEAN

Colorado R.

Arkansas R.

Red R.

Mississippi R.

Rio Grande

N

MEXICO

FLORIDA

Gulf of Mexico

NEW SPAIN

CUBA

0        500        1000 mi
0    500    1000 km

**193**

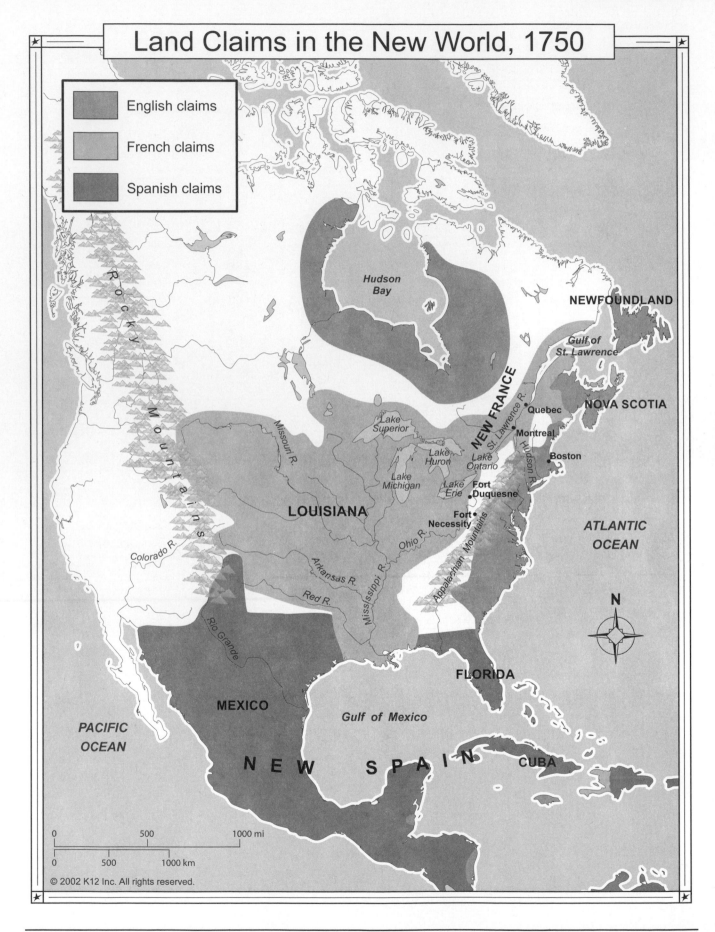

## Land Claims in the New World, 1750

English claims

French claims

Spanish claims

ROCKY Mountains

Hudson Bay

NEWFOUNDLAND

Gulf of St. Lawrence

NOVA SCOTIA

NEW FRANCE

St. Lawrence R.

Quebec

Montreal

Boston

Lake Superior

Missouri R.

Lake Huron

Lake Ontario

Lake Michigan

Lake Erie

Fort Duquesne

Hudson R.

LOUISIANA

Fort Necessity

Ohio R.

Appalachian Mountains

ATLANTIC OCEAN

Colorado R.

Arkansas R.

Mississippi R.

Red R.

N

Rio Grande

FLORIDA

MEXICO

Gulf of Mexico

PACIFIC OCEAN

N E W   S P A I N

CUBA

0    500    1000 mi

0    500    1000 km

© 2002 K12 Inc. All rights reserved.

Name _____     Date _____

## Talking Heads: Proclamation of 1763

These three heads represent Native Americans, colonists, and British officials. In each head, write a sentence, draw a picture, or make a symbol that states what that group thought about the Proclamation of 1763.

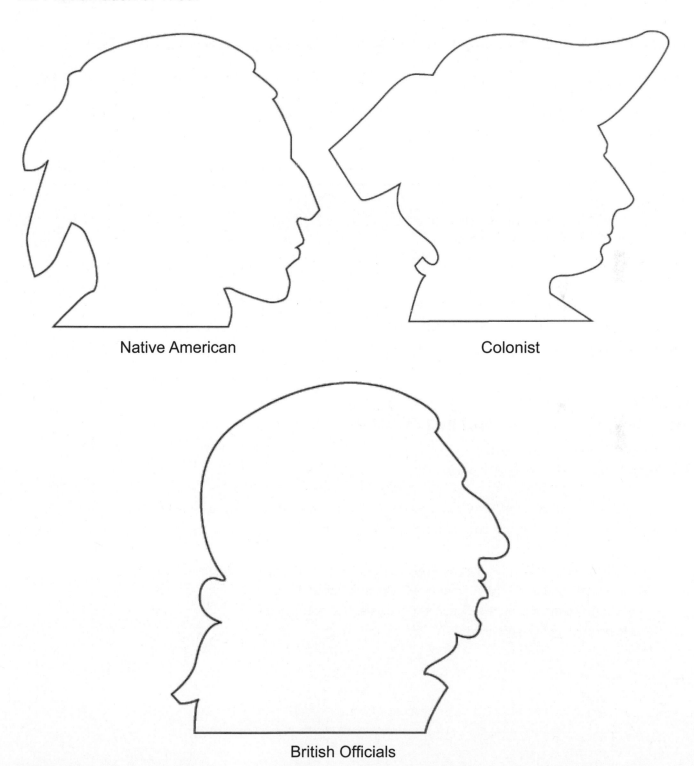

Native American

Colonist

British Officials

# Student Guide
## Lesson 4: (Optional) Boone Went Over the Mountain

Imagine heading into the wilderness on your own. You are going through native hunting grounds, so there is a threat of Indian attack. There is danger from wild animals as well. Would you keep pushing forward? Daniel Boone, one of the most famous pioneers in American history, dealt with these and many other hazards as he went deep into the American frontier.

Even though you may skip this lesson, you must complete the **Read On** section before moving on to the next lesson.

### Lesson Objectives
- Demonstrate mastery of important knowledge and skills taught in previous lessons.
- Analyze primary sources to gain information.
- Identify Daniel Boone as an early American pioneer.

# PREPARE

Approximate lesson time is 60 minutes.

### Materials
> For the Student
>> 📖 Document Analysis: Daniel Boone
>>
>> A History of US (Concise Edition), Volume A (Prehistory to 1800) by Joy Hakim
>>
>> History Journal

# LEARN
## Activity 1. Optional: Adventures of Daniel Boone (Offline)
### Instructions
### Use What You Know

Use your document analysis skills as you read Daniel Boone's own story. Do you remember what someone's journal or diary about an event is called? It's a *primary source.*

- Go online and visit Archiving Early America (http://www.earlyamerica.com/lives/boone/).
- Read Parts 1 and 2 of "The Adventures of Colonel Daniel Boone."
- Answer the questions on the Document Analysis: Daniel Boone sheet.
- Have an adult check your work.

## Read On

Americans believed English rights were their rights, rights the Magna Carta had given them in 1215. The English disagreed. This set the stage for a step-by-step progression of events that led to the American Revolution. Read Chapter 55, pages 258–260, and Chapter 56, pages 261–264. Meet King George III and begin the journey to revolution.

Vocabulary

You'll see these terms as you read. Write a brief definition for each term in your History Journal.

- Magna Carta
- habeas corpus
- repealed
- minister

Name _____     Date _____

## Document Analysis: Daniel Boone

After reviewing "The Adventures of Colonel Daniel Boon," answer the following questions.

1. Type of document (check one):

   _____ Newspaper      _____ Report

   _____ Letter          _____ Map

   _____ Telegram        _____ Journal/Diary

2. Date of document: _____

3. Author of document: _____

4. For what audience was the document written? _____

5. Why do you think Daniel Boone wrote this document? _____

   _____

6. List two things the document tells you about life on the Appalachian frontier at that time.

   _____

   _____

   _____

   _____

7. Do you think Daniel Boone gave a fair account of his run-ins with the Native Americans?
   Why or why not? _____

   _____

   _____

   _____

# Student Guide
## Lesson 5: The Stamp of English Rights

The English were used to conflict with their rulers. It helped build their government. But they weren't prepared for conflict with the colonists. After the British government tried to raise money by taxing stamps and tea, the colonists sent the British a message: "No taxation without representation."

## Lesson Objectives

- Explain the significance of Magna Carta and the "rights of Englishmen."
- Identify George III as the king of England in the mid-eighteenth century.
- Identify and describe the Stamp Act.
- Describe the reasons for and results of the Boston Tea Party.

---

# PREPARE

Approximate lesson time is 60 minutes.

## Materials

For the Student

🖳 Revolutionary Action and Reaction

A History of US (Concise Edition), Volume A (Prehistory to 1800) by Joy Hakim

History Journal

---

# LEARN
## Activity 1: Stamp It Out *(Offline)*
### Instructions
**Check Your Reading (Chapter 55, pages 258–260, and Chapter 56, pages 261–264)**

Check what you learned in Chapters 55 and 56 using the following questions.

1. Why is the Magna Carta so important in the history of democracy?
2. Why did George III and Parliament tax the colonies?
3. Why did taxes imposed by Britain anger the colonists?
4. How did the conflict over British taxes bring the colonies together?

---

**Use What You Know**

Complete the Revolutionary Action and Reaction sheet.

**Read On**

A *firebrand* is someone who stirs things up and gets people excited or angry. Three firebrands helped spark the war with their actions and words. From north to south, people soon knew the names of Samuel Adams, Thomas Paine, and Patrick Henry.

Draw a chart with three columns in your History Journal. At the top of each column, write the name of one of these leaders: Samuel Adams, Thomas Paine, and Patrick Henry.

Read Chapter 57, pages 265–270. As you read, look for ways in which these leaders were firebrands. On the chart, list the ways in which each leader was revolutionary.

**Beyond the Lesson**

Go back online to visit the Boston Tea Party website (http://www.pbs.org/ktca/liberty/chronicle_boston1774.html).

## Activity 2: The Stamp of English Rights *(Online)*

Name _____  Date _____

## Revolutionary Action and Reaction

Complete the action and reaction chart. You may need to fill in the action, date, or reaction for an event. You may use your book. The first two have been done for you.

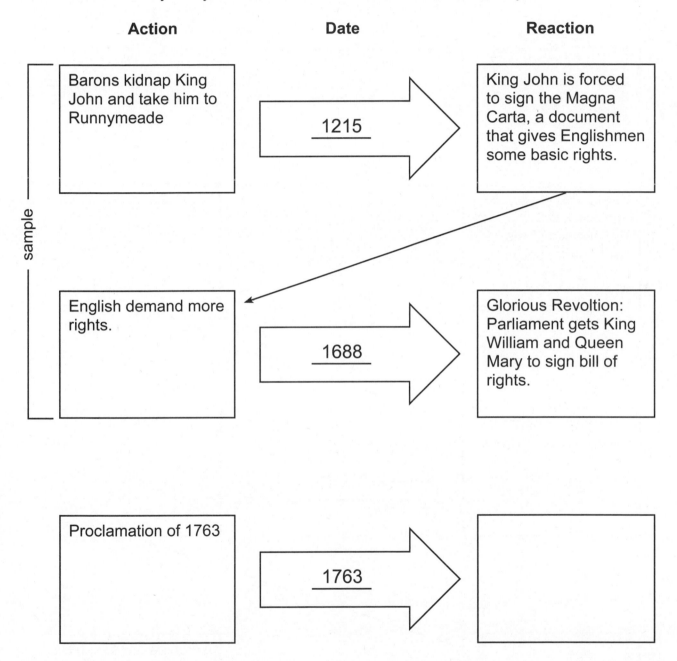

| Action | Date | Reaction |
|--------|------|----------|

**sample**

Barons kidnap King John and take him to Runnymeade — 1215 → King John is forced to sign the Magna Carta, a document that gives Englishmen some basic rights.

English demand more rights. — 1688 → Glorious Revoltion: Parliament gets King William and Queen Mary to sign bill of rights.

Proclamation of 1763 — 1763 →

| Action | Date | Reaction |
|--------|------|----------|

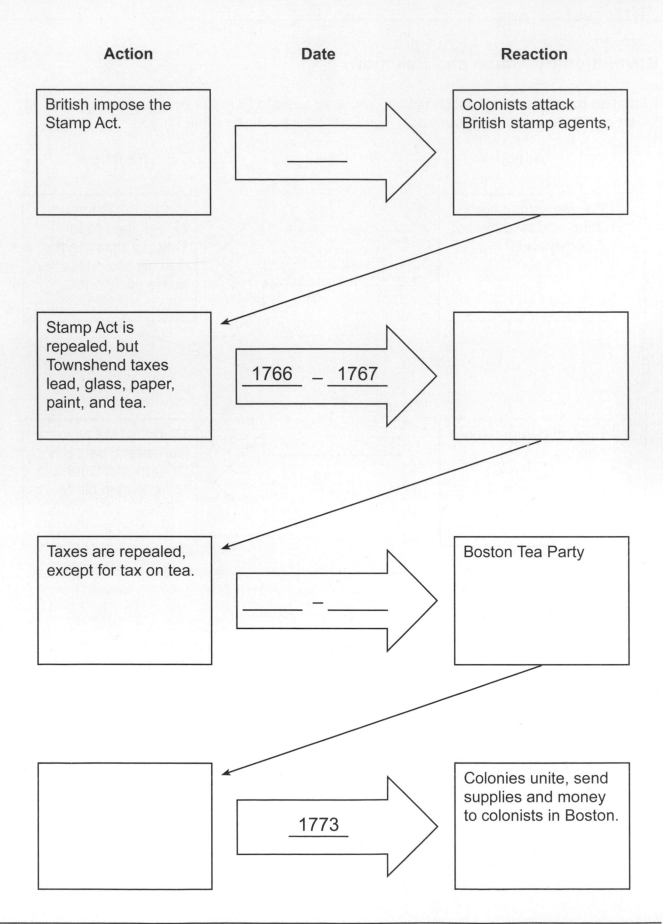

British impose the Stamp Act.

———

Colonists attack British stamp agents,

Stamp Act is repealed, but Townshend taxes lead, glass, paper, paint, and tea.

1766 – 1767

Taxes are repealed, except for tax on tea.

——— – ———

Boston Tea Party

1773

Colonies unite, send supplies and money to colonists in Boston.

# Student Guide
## Lesson 6: Give Us Liberty!

Words can be very powerful. Three fiery men used words and actions to help spark the Revolutionary War. People from north to south soon knew Samuel Adams, Thomas Paine, and Patrick Henry.

### Lesson Objectives
- Identify Sam Adams and Patrick Henry as opposition leaders.
- Analyze Patrick Henry's speech.

# PREPARE

Approximate lesson time is 60 minutes.

### Materials
For the Student

  🖥 Patrick Henry: Give Me Liberty or Give Me Death

  🖥 Some Detective Work

  A History of US (Concise Edition), Volume A (Prehistory to 1800) by Joy Hakim

  History Journal

# LEARN
## Activity 1: Liberty or Death *(Offline)*
### Instructions
**Check Your Reading (Chapter 57, pages 265–270)**
Discuss Chapter 57 with an adult, using the following questions:

1. How did firebrands such as Sam Adams help speed the flow of ideas?
2. What special talents helped make Sam Adams, Thomas Paine, and Patrick Henry effective firebrands?
3. What did Thomas Paine help make clear to colonists in his pamphlet *Common Sense?*
4. What did Patrick Henry mean when he said, "The war is actually begun"?

Complete the Some Detective Work sheet.
### Use What You Know

- Read Patrick Henry's "Give Me Liberty or Give Me Death" speech.
- Imagine you are a newspaper reporter from the *Virginia Gazette* and were in the church that night listening to Patrick Henry's speech. Write a newspaper story in your History Journal based on what you saw and heard that night. Be sure to include sounds and sights, not only from Patrick Henry, but from the crowd as well.

**Read On**

Massacre or tragic accident? Either way, citizens of Boston were killed by British soldiers on a cold March evening in 1770. Who would defend the soldiers in court? Would you have the courage to take the case when your neighbors are looking for revenge? And what should the colonies do as the situation worsenes?

Read Chapter 58, pages 271–275.

Vocabulary

You'll see these words as you read. Write a brief definition for each word in your History Journal.

- Patriot
- quarter
- Loyalist
- congress
- redcoat

Name _____          Date _____

## Some Detective Work

The year is 1770. The tension is rising between Britain and the American colonies. You have heard rumors that a revolution is in the works. The quotes below clue you in to the crisis at hand. Can you connect each quote with its speaker?
William Pitt Thomas Paine Benjamin Franklin

Sir William Johnson Patrick Henry


1. "If England is to become a great nation, she must go to school with the Iroquois."

   _____


2. "We have an old mother that peevish has grown,
   She snubs us like children that scarce walk alone,
   She forgets we're grown up and have sense of our own."

   _____


3. "I know not what course others may take, but as for me, give me liberty, or give me death!"

   _____


4. "This is the mother country, they are the children; they must obey, and we prescribe."

   _____


5. "Common Sense, Addressed to the Inhabitants of America . . . "

   _____

**Thinking Cap Question!** When Britain tried to enforce the Stamp Act, colonists let the world know that they hated the new tax, crying "No Taxation Without Representation." They even tarred and feathered commissioners for trying to collect the taxes. If Americans felt they were being unfairly taxed today, do you think they would protest? How?

Adapted from *A History of US*

Name _____ Date _____

## Patrick Henry: Give Me Liberty or Give Me Death

*Patrick Henry, March 23, 1775*

… I shall speak forth my sentiments freely and without reserve. This is no time for ceremony. The question before the House is one of awful moment to this country. For my own part, I consider it as nothing less than a question of freedom or slavery…

… I know of no way of judging of the future but by the past. And judging by the past, I wish to know what there has been in the conduct of the British ministry for the last ten years to justify those hopes with which gentlemen have been pleased to solace themselves… Are fleets and armies necessary to a work of love and reconciliation? Have we shown ourselves so unwilling to be reconciled that force must be called in to win back our love? Let us not deceive ourselves, sir. These are the implements of war and subjugation; the last arguments to which kings resort.

… If we wish to be free… we must fight! I repeat it, sir, we must fight! An appeal to arms and to the God of hosts is all that is left us!

… They tell us, sir, that we are weak; unable to cope with so formidable an adversary. But when shall we be stronger? Will it be the next week, or the next year? Will it be when we are totally disarmed, and when a British guard shall be stationed in every house?… Sir, we are not weak if we make a proper use of those means which the God of nature hath placed in our power. The millions of people, armed in the holy cause of liberty, and in such a country as that which we possess, are invincible by any force which our enemy can send against us.

There is no retreat but in submission and slavery! Our chains are forged! Their clanking may be heard on the plains of Boston! The war is inevitable—and let it come! I repeat it, sir, let it come.

… Gentlemen may cry, Peace, Peace—but there is no peace. The war is actually begun! The next gale that sweeps from the north will bring to our ears the clash of resounding arms! Our brethren are already in the field! Why stand we here idle? What is it that gentlemen wish? What would they have? Is life so dear, or peace so sweet, as to be purchased at the price of chains and slavery? Forbid it, Almighty God! I know not what course others may take; but as for me, give me liberty or give me death!

# *Student Guide*
## Lesson 7: The Boston Massacre

The Boston Massacre brought into sharp focus the colonists' growing frustration with British soldiers in America. The trial that followed highlighted John Adams's commitment to the belief that everyone deserves a fair trial. The debates in the First Continental Congress showed the quality of the leaders who would soon shape a new nation.

## Lesson Objectives

- Demonstrate mastery of important knowledge and skills taught in previous lessons.
- Analyze an artist's representation of the Boston Massacre.
- Identify John Adams as a Boston lawyer who defended the British soldiers after the Boston Massacre.
- Identify *Quartering Act* and *redcoat*.
- Identify George III as the king of England in the mid-eighteenth century.
- Identify and describe the Stamp Act.
- Identify Sam Adams and Patrick Henry as opposition leaders.
- Analyze Patrick Henry's speech.

---

# PREPARE

Approximate lesson time is 60 minutes.

## Materials

For the Student

🖳 The Midnight Rider

A History of US (Concise Edition), Volume A (Prehistory to 1800) by Joy Hakim

History Journal

---

# LEARN
## Activity 1: Massacre in Boston *(Offline)*
### Instructions
**Check Your Reading (Chapter 58, pages 271–275)**

Review Chapter 58.

Answer the following questions in complete sentences in your History Journal.

1. Why do you think the colonists didn't like the Quartering Act?
2. How did most of the British soldiers feel about being in America?
3. Who were the redcoats and why did John Adams take their case?
4. Did all of the representatives at the Continental Congress agree on what they should do about England? Explain.

---

**Use What You Know**

Complete the Midnight Rider sheet.

---

## ASSESS

### Lesson Assessment: The Boston Massacre (*Online*)

You will complete an online assessment covering the main objectives of this lesson. Your assessment will be scored by the computer.

Name _____     Date _____

## The Midnight Rider

Answer the questions by recalling information from your reading.

1. What famous horseback rider carved this engraving? _____

2. What notorious scene does it depict?

   _____

   _____

3. Who are the soldiers? Who are the civilians?

   _____

   _____

   _____

4. How is the engraving misleading?

   _____

   _____

   _____

5. Look up the word propaganda in the dictionary. In your own words, explain what propaganda is. _____

   _____

   _____

6. Was this engraving used as propaganda? By whom, and for what purpose?

   _____

   _____

   _____

   _____

Adapted from *A History of US*

# *Student Guide*
## Lesson 8: The Shot Heard Round the World

Fighting in Lexington and Concord between the redcoats and colonists pushed the colonies toward war and on the road to nationhood.

### Lesson Objectives

- Summarize the events at Lexington and Concord and explain the phrase "the shot heard round the world."
- Use a map to understand the battles of Lexington and Concord.

# PREPARE

Approximate lesson time is 60 minutes.

### Materials

For the Student

📖 Fight for Independence

A History of US (Concise Edition), Volume A (Prehistory to 1800) by Joy Hakim

History Journal

# LEARN
### Activity 1: Fight for Independence *(Offline)*
### Instructions
### Read

Conflict turned to war when the minutemen and redcoats scuffled at Lexington and Concord. The march toward nationhood had begun.

Read Chapter 59, pages 276–282, to learn about Paul Revere's ride and how it helped warn the colonists of a British attack.

Discuss the following questions with an adult:

1. What triggered the British march on Concord?
2. Why were Samuel Adams and John Hancock hiding in Lexington?
3. Why did the poet Ralph Waldo Emerson call the first bullet fired in Lexington "the shot heard round the world"?
4. What did the battles of Concord and Lexington prove about the colonists?

## Use What You Know

- Go back online and select the links to the Archiving Early America website to see two movies: *Paul Revere* ( http://earlyamerica.com/paul_revere.htm) and *The Shot Heard Round the World* (http://earlyamerica.com/shot_heard.htm).
- Complete the Fight for Independence sheet using information from your book and the two online movies.

Name _____   Date _____

## Fight for Independence

Write a brief description in each box of what happened at that location on the night of April 18, 1775. Use what you learned from your reading and from the movie clips at the Archiving Early America website to help you. Use the map key and draw the routes of Paul Revere, William Dawes, and Dr. Samuel Prescott on that famous night.

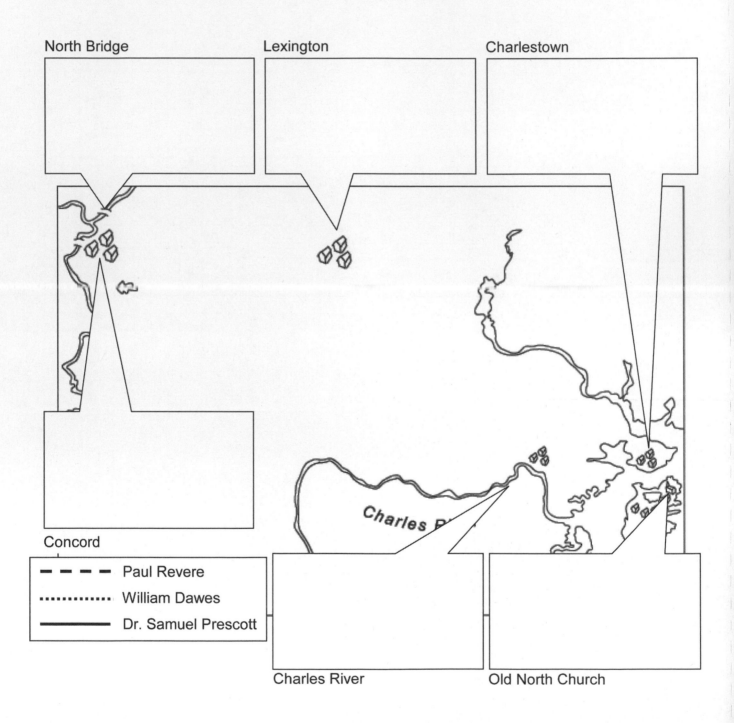

North Bridge

Lexington

Charlestown

Concord

Charles River

Old North Church

- - - - Paul Revere
··········· William Dawes
———— Dr. Samuel Prescott

Charles R

# Student Guide
## Lesson 9: Map Skills

In 1763, King George III issued a proclamation to keep the colonists east of the Appalachian Mountains. That same year, the French colony of New Orleans was given to the Spanish Empire. This port would play an important role in the coming war between the colonies and England.

Learn about the physical changes that have occurred in New Orleans over the past 200 years. Then read on to learn about the Second Continental Congress.

### Lesson Objectives

- Compare maps and tables to assess change over time.
- Define *elevation* as height above sea level.
- Identify major landforms in the United States.
- Use landform maps and relief maps to locate physical features.

# PREPARE

Approximate lesson time is 60 minutes.

### Materials

> For the Student
>> A History of US (Concise Edition), Volume A (Prehistory to 1800) by Joy Hakim
>> Understanding Geography: Map Skills and Our World (Level 5)
>> History Journal

# LEARN
## Activity 1: Mapping Change (Offline)
### Instructions
### Learn from Maps

Places change over time. New Orleans has changed dramatically over the past 200 years. People and the forces of nature have modified it. To learn about landforms and compare maps of New Orleans at different times:

- Complete Activity 5, "Landforms" (pages 20–23), and Activity 10, "Change Over Time: The Example of New Orleans" (pages 40–43), in *Understanding Geography*.
- Answer Questions 1–9 and 13–15 of Activity 5 in your History Journal. (Questions 10–12 and 16–19 are optional.)
- Answer Questions 1–12 of Activity 10 in your History Journal. (Questions 13–14 are optional.)
- If you have time, you may want to answer the Skill Builder Questions on pages 23 and 43. They are optional.
- After you have finished, compare your answers with the ones in the Learning Coach Guide.

# ASSESS

## Lesson Assessment: Map Skills (*Online*)

Answer the online geography questions covering the main goals of this lesson. Your assessment will be scored by the computer.

# Student Guide
## Lesson 10: A Continental Congress

When delegates to the Second Continental Congress met in Philadelphia, it became clear that they needed to choose a general to turn the raggedy militia into a powerful army. George Washington was the man for the job.

### Lesson Objectives

- Explain the purpose of the Second Continental Congress and describe the kinds of men who attended the Second Continental Congress as mostly educated, wealthy and prominent.
- Explain the reasons for choosing George Washington to command the Continental Army, including his experience and character.

# PREPARE

Approximate lesson time is 60 minutes.

### Materials

For the Student

    📖 Who's Who at the Second Continental Congress

    A History of US (Concise Edition), Volume A (Prehistory to 1800) by Joy Hakim

    History Journal

# LEARN
## Activity 1: The Second Continental Congress *(Offline)*
### Instructions
### Read

Few of the delegates who traveled to Philadelphia in 1775 wanted to rush headlong into revolution. However, with musket balls flying in Boston, most wondered how long they could continue to call themselves English subjects. How did they make such a difficult decision?

The delegates assigned the task of shaping a raggedy militia into a Continental Army to George Washington. When King George III rejected the Olive Branch Petition, Washington knew the war would go on. But could he have imagined he would not go home for nearly eight years?

Read Chapter 60, pages 283–289, and Chapter 61, pages 290–292. As you read, complete the Who's Who at the Second Continental Congress sheet.

Name _____          Date _____

## Who's Who at the Second Continental Congress

For each delegate at the Second Continental Congress, fill in the colony he represented and any important facts that tell you what kind of man he was. For example, was the delegate rich or poor? What kind of education did he have? Was he well known in the colony he came from? What accomplishments was he best known for?

| Delegate | Colony | Important Facts |
|---|---|---|
| George Washington | | |
| Richard Henry Lee | | |
| Phillip Livingston | | |
| Joseph Hewes | | |
| Stephen Hopkins | | |
| Benjamin Franklin | | |
| John Adams | | |
| John Hancock | | |
| Thomas Jefferson | | |

# Student Guide
## Lesson 11: The Fighting Begins

As the delegates to the Second Continental Congress were meeting in Philadelphia, the first major battle occurred at Breed's Hill and Bunker Hill.

## Lesson Objectives

- Describe the battle at Breed's Hill and Bunker Hill and explain its significance as demonstrating the colonists' ability to fight.

---

# PREPARE

Approximate lesson time is 60 minutes.

## Materials

For the Student

📖 Who? What? When? Where? Why?

A History of US (Concise Edition), Volume A (Prehistory to 1800) by Joy Hakim

History Journal

---

# LEARN
## Activity 1: The Revolution Begins (Offline)
### Instructions
### Read

Read Chapter 62, pages 293–297. (Do not read the feature on the Age of Enlightenment; you will read that in the next lesson.) Then complete the Who? What? When? Where? Why? sheet.

Name _____    Date _____

## Who? What? When? Where? Why?

Can you summon up the answers to these questions?

1. **WHO?** They were asleep on that June night in 1775 as Massachusetts soldiers dug in fortifications on Breed's Hill. Who were they?

   _____

2. **WHAT?** What river did the British cross to get from Boston to Charlestown?

   _____

3. **WHERE?** A famous battle took place in this lady's hairdo! What were the names of the hills on which the fighting took place?

   _____

4. **WHEN?** What were the American soldiers instructed to hold fire until they saw?

   _____

5. **WHY?** Why did they hold fire until the last minute?

   _____

**Thinking Cap Question!** Imagine you were one of the soldiers who fought in the battle pictured above. Write a diary entry describing what happened to you that day.

# Student Guide
## Lesson 12: Will You Sign?

The Declaration of Independence introduced the world to the American idea of representative government. Its focus on equality and natural rights has guided generations of Americans.

## Lesson Objectives

- Demonstrate mastery of important knowledge and skills in previous lessons.
- Summarize Thomas Paine's arguments for independence.
- Explain how Thomas Jefferson was chosen to write the Declaration of Independence.
- Recognize the Enlightenment ideas Jefferson used in the Declaration of Independence.
- Summarize the events at Lexington and Concord and explain the phrase "the shot heard round the world."
- Explain the reasons for choosing George Washington to command the Continental Army, including his experience and character.
- Describe the battle at Breed's Hill and Bunker Hill and explain its significance as demonstrating the colonists' ability to fight.

---

# PREPARE

Approximate lesson time is 60 minutes.

## Materials

For the Student

    📖 Age of Enlightenment

    A History of US (Concise Edition), Volume A (Prehistory to 1800) by Joy Hakim

    History Journal

    📖 Will You Sign? Assessment Sheet

---

# LEARN
## Activity 1: Declaring Independence (Offline)
### Instructions
### Discuss

Do you remember when you read about the "firebrands"? One of those firebrands, Thomas Paine, made his mark around this time. Paine came to America from England and helped the colonists say what was really in their hearts. Paine's pamphlet, *Common Sense*, stated clearly that the colonies must be free from England. In its first three months, *Common Sense* sold 120,000 copies in the colonies. It stressed three points:

1. Monarchy was a poor form of government, and the colonies would be better off without it.
2. Great Britain was hurting the colonies' economy with taxes and trade restrictions.
3. It was foolish for a small island 3,000 miles away to try to rule a whole continent.

---

Discuss Thomas Paine's arguments for independence with an adult.

### Read

Read the feature in Chapter 62 titled, "How the New World Changed the Old, and Vice Versa," and complete the Age of Enlightenment sheet.

Read Chapter 63, pages 298–302, and answer the following questions in your History Journal.

1. What was the goal of the people who signed the Declaration of Independence?
2. Why was Thomas Jefferson chosen to write the Declaration of Independence?
3. What three things did the delegates want Jefferson to accomplish in the Declaration?
4. The author wants to know: What does *equal* mean?
5. What Enlightenment ideas did Jefferson use in the Declaration of Independence?

### Look Back

Go back online and review previous lessons with the flash cards to prepare for the assessment.

### Assessment

You will take an offline assessment.

---

# ASSESS
## Mid-Unit Assessment: Will You Sign? (*Offline*)
You will complete an offline Mid-Unit Assessment. An adult will score the assessment and enter the results online.

---

Name _____    Date _____

## The Age of Enlightenment

Fill in the blanks with terms from the word bank below. Some terms may be used more than once. Refer to the feature in Chapter 62, partially quoted below, if you need help.

| | | |
|---|---|---|
| Enlightenment | John Locke | Jean-Jacques Rousseau |
| people | rulers | House of Burgesses |
| democratic government | natural rights | Isaac Newton |
| governments | superstition | assemblies | raw materials |

Lights were being lit in the eighteenth century—so many lights that it would come to be

called a time of _____. The lights were going on in the minds of the

thinking people. Some of the electricity for those lights had come from a scientist named

_____. He had shown that the universe was not as full of mystery as

people had supposed. It could be understood with study and observation and by people

using their brains. That was an astonishing thought in a world that had often been guided

by _____ and fear. Suddenly there seemed to be all kinds of brilliant

thinkers who were using their minds and encouraging others to do the same thing.

An Englishman named _____ and a Frenchman named

_____ were two of the most important Enlightenment thinkers.

They thought about politics and the way _____ were run....

_____ wrote about _____. He said

that governments should be run for the _____, not for their

_____. He made people think about democracy....

The colonists knew something else: they knew they could govern themselves. They didn't need kings or nobles to make decisions for them. Americans had been running their own _____ for years. There was the General Court in Massachusetts, the _____ in Virginia, and lawmaking bodies in each colony. Nowhere in Europe did people have that kind of experience in self-government . . . .

Americans were sending _____ to England—like lumber and tobacco—and getting them sent back as finished goods—furniture and cigars. Well, another raw material got sent back and forth across the sea: the idea of freedom and _____.

Assessment

American History A – Unit 5: Road to Revolution
Lesson 12: Will You Sign?

Name _____  Date _____

## Mid-Unit Assessment

1. What did the poet Emerson mean by "the shot heard round the world"?

   _____

   _____

   _____

2. True or False? American minutemen forced the British redcoats to retreat from Concord, Massachusetts. _____

3. Why did Paul Revere and William Dawes ride toward Lexington on the night of April 18, 1775?

   _____

   _____

4. John Adams believed that the experience and character of one particular person made him the right man to be commander in chief of the Continental Army. Who was this man?

   _____

5. Why did the American officers tell the volunteers not to fire "until you see the whites of their eyes"? _____

   _____

6. True or False? The battle at Breed's Hill and Bunker Hill was a terrible defeat for the Americans and many Americans lost confidence. _____

7. Who wrote *Common Sense*? _____

8. True or False? Thomas Jefferson was chosen to write the Declaration of Independence because he was one of the oldest and most talkative men at the Second Continental Congress. _____

⚙ Assessment

American History A – Unit 5: Road to Revolution
Lesson 12: Will You Sign?

9. In the Declaration of Independence, Thomas Jefferson included Enlightenment ideas

such as those of the English philosopher _____ , who wrote about
natural rights.

10. What was the main idea presented in *Common Sense*?

_____

_____

11. True or False: Most of the men who attended the Second Continental Congress were rich

landowners. _____

# Student Guide
## Lesson 13: Life, Liberty, and the Pursuit of Happiness

The Declaration of Independence stated clearly that colonists were breaking away from England. It was a very bold statement. Fifty-six men signed the document.

### Lesson Objectives
- Read and analyze the Declaration of Independence to gain understanding of its meaning.

---

# PREPARE

Approximate lesson time is 60 minutes.

### Materials

For the Student

    📖 Guided Reading: Declaration of Independence

    A History of US (Concise Edition), Volume A (Prehistory to 1800) by Joy Hakim

    History Journal

---

# LEARN
## Activity 1: Understanding the Declaration (Offline)
### Instructions
### Read

Follow the instructions on the Guided Reading: Declaration of Independence sheet as you read sections of the Declaration of Independence in the book's appendix.

#### Optional: Beyond the Lesson
See what went on in Philadelphia during the summer of 1776. Visit Archiving Early America: Declaring Independence (http://earlyamerica.com/independence.htm).

## Activity 2. Optional: The Summer of 1776 (Online)

---

Name _____    Date _____

## Guided Reading: The Declaration of Independence

Complete this sheet as you read sections 1–4 of the Declaration of Independence. It is located in the book's appendix.

I.   Preamble

Read the first paragraph of the Declaration of Independence.

1.  This long first sentence is called the Preamble, which means "introduction." What country does Thomas Jefferson say the people of the colonies must break away from?

_____

2.  When Jefferson says Americans "should declare the causes which impel them to the Separation," he means they should state to the world why they are forced to become independent. Why do you think he says that they should explain this to the whole world?

_____

_____

II.  Philosophy

Read the first sentence of the second paragraph that begins with "We hold…"

3.  What does Jefferson say about human beings? _____

_____

4.  What rights does the Declaration of Independence say that all people are born with?

_____

_____

_____

Read the next sentence that begins with "That to secure…"

5.  According to the Declaration, governments exist in order to do what? _____

_____

6. Where do governments get their power? _____

7. What should the people do when a government does not protect their rights?

_____

## III. Grievances

8. Jefferson lists the destructive things King George III has done to the colonies. You don't need to read them unless you would like to, but you might find it interesting to count them and see how many crimes are mentioned. Start with the sentence beginning, "He has refused his assent…" Count every paragraph that begins with the word "he" or "for" and see how many you find by the time you see the one that begins, "He has excited domestic

Insurrections…" How many complaints are there? _____

## IV. Declaration

Read the paragraph that begins with "We, therefore…"

9. Jefferson wrote, "these United Colonies are, and by Right ought to be, FREE AND INDEPENDENT STATES; that they are absolved from all Allegiance to the British Crown…" Rewrite that sentence in your own words.

_____

_____

10. What did the signers promise to each other? What does it mean in your own words?

_____

_____

11. Who was the first person to sign the Declaration of Independence?

_____

# *Student Guide*
## Lesson 14: Unit Review

You've completed Unit 5, Road to Revolution. It's time to review what you've learned. You'll take the Unit Assessment in the next lesson.

(This review might refer to topics presented in optional lessons in this unit.)

### Lesson Objectives

- Summarize the ideas and events leading to the American Revolution.

---

# PREPARE

Approximate lesson time is 60 minutes.

### Materials

  For the Student

  A History of US (Concise Edition), Volume A (Prehistory to 1800) by Joy Hakim

  History Journal

---

# LEARN
## Activity 1: A Look Back *(Offline)*
### Instructions
### Online Review

Use the following to review this unit online:

- The Big Picture
- Time Line
- Flash Cards

History Journal Review

Review more by going through your History Journal. Look at the worksheets you completed for this unit. Review your vocabulary words. If you completed writing assignments, read them. Don't rush through; take your time. Your History Journal is a great resource for a unit review.

# Student Guide
## Lesson 15: Unit Assessment

You've finished this unit! Take the unit assessment. Then read on for the next lesson.

## Lesson Objectives

- Analyze the wisdom of Benjamin Franklin and apply it to today.
- Explain the causes of the French and Indian War as competition between France and England for land and power.
- Identify George Washington as a soldier in the British Army during the French and Indian War.
- Describe the problems the British government faced after 1763 in trying to limit westward migration and why many Americans wanted to go west.
- Locate the Appalachian Mountains on a map and explain that the British did not want migration across them for reasons of economics and security.
- Explain the significance of Magna Carta and the "rights of Englishmen."
- Identify and describe the Stamp Act.
- Analyze Patrick Henry's speech.
- Identify John Adams as a Boston lawyer who defended the British soldiers after the Boston Massacre.
- Summarize the events at Lexington and Concord and explain the phrase "the shot heard round the world."
- Explain the purpose of the Second Continental Congress and describe the kinds of men who attended the Second Continental Congress as mostly educated, wealthy and prominent.
- Explain the reasons for choosing George Washington to command the Continental Army, including his experience and character.
- Summarize Thomas Paine's arguments for independence.
- Explain how Thomas Jefferson was chosen to write the Declaration of Independence.
- Recognize the Enlightenment ideas Jefferson used in the Declaration of Independence.
- Read and analyze the Declaration of Independence to gain understanding of its meaning.
- Identify the Boston Massacre as a clash between colonists and British soldiers.

---

# PREPARE

Approximate lesson time is 60 minutes.

## Materials

For the Student

📖 Road to Revolution Assessment Sheet

A History of US (Concise Edition), Volume A (Prehistory to 1800) by Joy Hakim

History Journal

---

# ASSESS
## Unit Assessment: Road to Revolution (*Offline*)
Complete the offline Unit Assessment. Your Learning Coach will score it and enter the results online.

# LEARN
## Activity 1: Chapters 64 and 65 *(Offline)*
### Instructions
### Read On

Read Chapter 64, pages 303–305, and Chapter 65, pages 306–310. Prepare to explain what effect the signing of the Declaration of Independence had on many of the colonists. Also prepare to describe the roles of women during the Revolution.

Name_____ Date_____

# Unit Assessment

**(2 points)**

1. Describe the major factors leading to the French and Indian War. (Write your answer using complete sentences.)

_____

_____

_____

_____

**(2 points)**

2. What problems did Britain face at the end of the French and Indian War? (Write your answer using complete sentences.)

_____

_____

_____

_____

3. Match each person or term on the left with a description on the right. Write the correct letter on the blank line.

_____ Boston Massacre

_____ Magna Carta

_____ Patrick Henry

_____ Stamp Act

**A.** A tax to be paid on every piece of printed paper

**B.** Member of the Virginia House of Burgesses who said, "Give me liberty or give me death!"

**C.** Document that gave the English many rights they had been denied

**D.** Engraver whose drawing depicted the Boston Massacre

**E.** Early conflict where five colonists were killed by British soldiers

4. What did Benjamin Franklin's famous political cartoon urge the colonists to do?

Ⓐ "Join, or Die"

Ⓑ "Fight the British"

Ⓒ "Vote for Washington"

Ⓓ "Join the Army"

5. He was a soldier for the British in the French and Indian War. Later, he went on to be in charge of the Continental Army. Who was he?

Ⓐ John Hancock

Ⓑ Benjamin Franklin

Ⓒ George Washington

Ⓓ Patrick Henry

6. Which one of the following was a major battle in the French and Indian War?

Ⓐ Battle of Quebec

Ⓑ Battle of Bunker Hill

Ⓒ Boston Massacre

Ⓓ Lexington and Concord

7. The British issued this order to stop colonists from migrating across the Allegheny Mountains.

Ⓐ Stamp Tax

Ⓑ Proclamation of 1763

Ⓒ Emancipation Proclamation

Ⓓ Magna Carta

8. He started the committees of correspondence to keep the colonies talking with each other.

Ⓐ King George III

Ⓑ Thomas Paine

Ⓒ George Washington

Ⓓ Sam Adams

9. What was the name of Thomas Paine's famous pamphlet?

(A) *Common Sense*

(B) *Glorious Revolution*

(C) Magna Carta

(D) Declaration of Independence

10. Whom did John Adams defend at the trial for the Boston Massacre?

(A) colonists

(B) British soldiers

(C) Indians

(D) slaves

11. Where was the "shot heard round the world" fired?

(A) Philadelphia

(B) Boston

(C) Lexington

(D) Williamsburg

12. Which of these men was **NOT** at the Second Continental Congress?

(A) Thomas Jefferson

(B) John Locke

(C) Benjamin Franklin

(D) John Adams

13. When Jefferson wrote the Declaration of Independence, he used the ideas of

philosophers from _____ .

(A) the Age of Enlightenment

(B) the Middle Ages

(C) the Industrial Age

(D) the Age of Exploration

14. Which of the following rights were guaranteed in the Declaration of Independence?

   (A) life

   (B) liberty

   (C) the pursuit of happiness

   (D) all of the above

15. Why was Thomas Jefferson chosen to write the Declaration of Independence?

   (A) He had the best handwriting.

   (B) Members of the Second Continental Congress knew he was a good writer.

   (C) He was eager to volunteer his services, and no one else wanted to write it.

   (D) He was one of the oldest members of the Continental Congress.

*(2 points)*

16. Describe at least two major points of the Declaration of Independence. (Write your answer using complete sentences.)

_____

_____

_____

_____

# Student Guide
## Lesson 1: John and Abigail Adams

How did a loosely knit group of colonies defeat the most powerful military in the world? Or did they? One biography of Washington gives him the credit for making the cost of a British victory too high. How? And what social and political changes occurred as a result of the war?

John Adams never gave up on independence. His hard work and the words of the Declaration of Independence finally convinced people to unify and fight for liberty. The men who fought were not alone. Women played an important part in the American Revolution, too. They served on the home front and on the battlefront. Their experiences during the war got them thinking about equality and liberty.

### Lesson Objectives
- Recognize John Adams's role in declaring independence as one of early and persistent support.
- Explain the significance of the Declaration of Independence in unifying people for the war effort.
- Describe the roles of women during the Revolution, including maintaining farms and businesses, assisting in the war effort, fighting, and being politically vocal.

---

# PREPARE

Approximate lesson time is 60 minutes.

## Materials
For the Student

🖳 Mail Bag!

A History of US (Concise Edition), Volume A (Prehistory to 1800) by Joy Hakim

History Journal

---

# LEARN
## Activity 1: Revolutionary Women and Children (Offline)
### Instructions
**Check Your Reading (Chapter 64, pages 303–305, and Chapter 65, pages 306–310)**

- Go over what you learned in Chapters 64 and 65.
- Complete the Mail Bag sheet. Have an adult check your answers.

**Discuss**

John Adams played an important role in getting the delegates to sign the Declaration of Independence. He was an early and persistent supporter of independence. He stood up for what he believed, even though he knew it could mean his life.

---

Have you ever believed strongly in something? Did you stand up for what you believed in? How far would you go in defending your beliefs?

Discuss the idea of standing up for what you believe with an adult.

**Use What You Know**

Write a list of "did you know" questions about women in the Revolution in your History Journal. Include the interesting, sometimes little-known facts mentioned in the book. For example: Did you know that women ran the family farms when their husbands went off to fight?

When you have finished, quiz your friends and family.

**Read On**

Would slaves fight in a revolution for a nation that allowed slavery? Would they side with the British? Would either side allow slaves to fight at all?

Read Chapter 66, pages 311–315, and Chapter 67, pages 316–317. Prepare to discuss how a black person or a woman of 1776 might have interpreted this phrase from the Declaration of Independence: "All men are created equal."

**Optional: Beyond the Lesson**

Join the signers in an interactive activity at the National Archives website (www.archives.gov/exhibit_hall/charters_of_freedom/declaration/join_the_signers/join_the_signers.html)

# Activity 2. Optional: Signers of the Declaration of Independence *(Online)*

Name _____     Date _____

## Mail Bag!

TO MR. JOHN ADAMS:

"In the new code of laws… I desire you remember the ladies…
if particular care and attention are not paid to the ladies we are
determined to foment a rebellion and will not hold ourselves bound
to obey any laws in which we have no voice or representation."

1. Who wrote this angry letter to John Adams? _____

2. What were women left in charge of when their husbands went to war? _____

_____

3. What were some of the things women did during the war? _____

_____

_____

4. Did any women fight on the battlefields of the Revolution? How? _____

_____

5. Do you think women started to become politically vocal during the war? Why or why not?

_____

_____

6. What is the name of the woman in the picture above? (Hint: She was famous for bringing

water to thirsty patriot soldiers.) _____

Use the Benjamin Banneker to Thomas Jefferson feature in Chapter 64 to answer the
following questions.

7. How were Benjamin Banneker and Thomas Jefferson alike? _____

_____

8. In your own words, what does Benjamin Banneker hope Thomas Jefferson will do?

_____

_____

Adapted from *A History of US*

# Student Guide
## Lesson 2: Decisions

People of African ancestry in the colonies understood very well the limits on equality. Some accepted offers of freedom from the British. Others fought to plant the seeds of racial freedom in their own land. And in Virginia, people had to choose to rebel or support the king when the royal governor proclaimed that "all indentured servants, Negroes, and others" were free if they were willing to defend the crown.

### Lesson Objectives
- Summarize the dilemma many blacks faced in taking sides during the Revolution.
- Describe the roles of blacks on both sides of the conflict.

# PREPARE

Approximate lesson time is 60 minutes.

### Materials
For the Student
- More Mail

A History of US (Concise Edition), Volume A (Prehistory to 1800) by Joy Hakim

History Journal

# LEARN
## Activity 1: Liberty for All? *(Offline)*
### Instructions
Check Your Reading (Chapter 66, pages 311–315, and Chapter 67, pages 316–317)

- Go over what you learned in Chapters 66 and 67.
- Complete the More Mail sheet. Have an adult check your answers.

### Discuss

The Declaration of Independence and the American Revolution influenced attitudes in the United States. They changed people's ideas of equality in ways that the Continental Congress did not intend. Discuss some of these changes with an adult.

**Use What You Know**

Choose one of the following activities to complete.

- Write a short newspaper article that explains the roles of blacks on both sides of the Revolutionary War.
- Imagine you are an African American or a woman in 1776. Write a letter to the editor of a newspaper expressing your interpretation of the Declaration of Independence.

Discuss your writing with an adult.

**Read On**

American colonists were not the only ones to fight for independence in the Continental Army. Many foreign soldiers came to America to help the colonies in their war with Britain. What were some of the reasons these men took part in the Revolution?

Read Chapter 68, pages 318–321. Be prepared to name two soldiers who fought on the side of the colonists, but were from another country.

**Optional: Beyond the Lesson**

Follow the directions online to learn more about James Forten.

# Activity 2. Optional: James Forten *(Online)*

Name _____ Date _____

## More Mail

TO GOVERNOR GAGE OF MASSACHUSETTS:

"We have in common with all other men a natural right to our freedoms… we are a freeborn people and have never forfeited this blessing by any compact or agreement whatever. But we were unjustly dragged by the cruel hand of power from our dearest friends and some of us stolen from… our tender parents and from a populous, pleasant and plentiful country and brought hither to be made slaves for life."

1. What did the authors of this letter claim to have in common with other men? _____

   _____

2. How were slaves collected and brought to America? _____

   _____

3. Many African-American men fought in the Revolutionary War. Why did this frighten many

   white Southerners? _____

   _____

4. What happened to Thomas Jefferson's slaves after they were carried off by British

   troops? _____

   _____

5. What did the African-American patriot soldier James Forten refuse to do for the British

   captain? _____

   _____

6. Why was the idea of equality radical in the 1770s? _____

   _____

Adapted from *A History of US*

# Student Guide
## Lesson 3: Best Friends

People from many nations were drawn into the conflict between Britain and the newly formed United States. These people contributed many things to the colonists' fight for liberty and independence: leadership, money, and even their lives.

### Lesson Objectives

- Demonstrate mastery of important knowledge and skills taught in previous lessons.
- Identify individuals who came from Europe to aid the American cause, including the Marquis de Lafayette, Baron Friedrich von Steuben, and Haym Salomon.
- Use research skills to gain information on one of the people mentioned in this lesson.
- Recognize John Adams's role in declaring independence as one of early and persistent support.
- Explain the significance of the Declaration of Independence in unifying people for the war effort.
- Describe the roles of women during the Revolution, including maintaining farms and businesses, assisting in the war effort, fighting, and being politically vocal.
- Summarize the dilemma many blacks faced in taking sides during the Revolution.

---

# PREPARE

Approximate lesson time is 60 minutes.

### Materials

For the Student

A History of US (Concise Edition), Volume A (Prehistory to 1800) by Joy Hakim

History Journal

🖳 Best Friends Assessment Sheet

---

# LEARN
## Activity 1: Soldiers from Everywhere (Offline)
### Instructions
**Check Your Reading (Chapter 68, pages 318–321)**

Discuss Chapter 68 with an adult. Then, play the "Who Is It?" game.

1. Using information from Chapter 68, fill four index cards with information about the following people, one card per person:

- Marquis de Lafayette
- Baron Friedrich von Steuben
- Haym Salomon
- Robert Morris

---

2. Ask an adult to read each card to you and see if you can remember who each person is. Here's an example:

"This man wrote the Declaration of Independence. He was one of the youngest members of the Continental Congress. He was tall and shy with red hair. He lived in Virginia. Who is it?" (Thomas Jefferson)

**Use What You Know**

Research one of the people you read about:

- Marquis de Lafayette
- Baron Friedrich von Steuben
- Haym Salomon
- Robert Morris

Use nonfiction books, encyclopedias (in print or online), and websites. Take notes during your research.

Use the information you gathered to write a commendation for the person you selected. In this sense, a *commendation* is a piece of writing that praises something, or many things, the person has done.

**Assessment**

After you complete the written assessment, an adult will enter the results online.

**Read On**

Now that the colonies had declared their independence, they had a war to fight. And unless they won, the Declaration of Independence would mean nothing. General Washington would face many problems. And although things didn't go well in the beginning, one major victory would turn things around for the Americans.

Read Chapter 69, pages 322–328. Be prepared to describe the difficulties George Washington faced as commander of the Continental Army, and name the battle that was a turning point in the war.

Vocabulary

You'll see the following terms as you read. Write a brief definition for each in your History Journal.

- Hessian
- mercenary

# ASSESS

## Mid-Unit Assessment: Best Friends (*Offline*)

You will complete an offline Mid-Unit Assessment covering the main goals for Lessons 1, 2, and 3. An adult will score the assessment and enter the results online.

Name _____     Date _____

# Mid-Unit Assessment

1.  How was John Adams helpful in getting the delegates to sign the Declaration of Independence?

    (A) He used violence and threats against those opposed to independence.

    (B) He talked persistently and convincingly about independence.

    (C) He promised them that the French would help if they signed the Declaration.

    (D) He included a section on the cruelty and immorality of slavery.

2.  What effect did the signing of the Declaration of Independence have on the colonists?

    (A) It filled them with pride and unified them.

    (B) It made them want to rebel against the delegates.

    (C) It filled them with disappointment.

    (D) It caused them to question their desire for independence.

3.  What was promised to slaves that encouraged them to fight for the British?

    (A) land

    (B) money

    (C) freedom

    (D) education

4.  Which of the following is a reason why more than 5,000 blacks fought on the American side during the Revolutionary War?

    (A) Those who were slaves would be able to rebel against their owners.

    (B) They believed in the words of the Declaration of Independence.

    (C) They believed George III would give them their freedom.

    (D) They were promised land and money.

5. Match each person on the left with the description on the right. (There is one extra description on the right that does not match any of the people on the left.)

_____ Baron Friedrich von Steuben

_____ Marquis de Lafayette

_____ Haym Salomon

_____ Abigail Adams

_____ John Hancock

_____ Mercy Otis Warren

A. This patriot signed the Declaration with a large, bold signature. He was the first delegate to sign.

B. This patriot became the American ambassador to France. He tried to persuade France to help America.

C. This former Prussian captain turned a disorderly group of American recruits into skilled soldiers.

D. This Polish Jew spied on the British in New York for the Patriots. The French later made him the paymaster for their army in America.

E. This wife of a delegate wrote letters to her husband about the inequality of women and blacks.

F. This Frenchman became a general on George Washington's staff. He became lifelong friends with Washington.

G. This woman wrote a play about the British. She used her writing to turn Loyalists into Patriots.

6. Name three ways American women helped during the Revolution.

_____

_____

_____

7. Explain how American women were able to fight as soldiers during the Revolution.

_____

_____

_____

# Student Guide
## Lesson 4: Challenges for the Continental Army

The opening battles of the Revolutionary War went badly for George Washington. He was sometimes forced to focus more on avoiding capture than on victory. But victories did come. The American victory at Saratoga changed the course of the war. Seeing the possibility of victory, the French joined the conflict on the side of the Americans.

## Lesson Objectives

- Define *Hessian* and *mercenary*.
- Identify Sir William Howe as the commander in charge of all the British forces in America.
- Describe the difficulties George Washington faced as commander of the Continental Army, including a small, unstable army, lack of supplies, and need to use retreat as a way to save the army.
- Analyze a painting, *Washington Crossing the Delaware,* to assess historical accuracy and bias.
- Explain the significance of the battles of Trenton and Saratoga (one boosted American morale; the other was a turning point in the war).

---

# PREPARE

Approximate lesson time is 60 minutes.

## Materials

For the Student

A History of US (Concise Edition), Volume A (Prehistory to 1800) by Joy Hakim

History Journal

---

# LEARN
## Activity 1: A Shaky Start, Then Victory *(Offline)*
### Instructions
### Check Your Reading (Chapter 69, pages 322–328)
Use the flash cards to review your reading. Then discuss the following with an adult.

1. What hardships did soldiers face early in the war?
2. What was Washington's strategy in the early battles waged in New York?
3. Who were the Hessians, and why did their use by the British anger many Americans?
4. Why were each of the following battles important to the American cause: the Battle of Trenton, the Battle of Princeton, and the Battle of Saratoga?

## Use What You Know

Imagine you're George Washington. It's 1776. In your History Journal:

- Make a list of the problems you are having as you try to fight the war.
- Make a list of the kinds of help you would like to get from France.

When you've finished, go back to the lesson online and click the link to view the painting *Washington Crossing the Delaware*.

- Look closely at the painting. Is it historically accurate? See if you can find any inaccuracies. There are five errors that are often observed.
- Do you see any bias in the way the painter shows this event? In other words, do you think the painter was influenced by his feelings and emotions toward the subject of his painting? If so, in what ways? How did this come out in the painting?

## Read On

In 1777, the British captured Philadelphia. Before that, General Washington lost two battles in Pennsylvania. Things weren't going well for the Americans. But things were about to change. Although no battles were fought at Valley Forge, and there was terrible suffering, something very good happened there. What was it?

Read Chapter 70, pages 329–335. Be prepared to name two important American military leaders of the Revolution, not including George Washington.

# Student Guide
## Lesson 5: Turning Points

The hardships of war gave Washington a battle-tested army. After Valley Forge, these troops began a campaign to sweep the British and their mercenaries off the continent.

## Lesson Objectives

- Locate the following places on a map: Saratoga, Philadelphia, Valley Forge, and Vincennes.
- Identify Martha Washington as providing moral support and Nathaniel Greene and George Rogers Clark as significant military leaders of the Revolution.
- Describe conditions at Valley Forge and summarize the significance of the winter there.
- Explain the reasons for the warfare on the frontier and the effect of the Revolution on Native Americans.
- Identify George Washington as providing example, dignity and determination to his army.

# PREPARE

Approximate lesson time is 60 minutes.

## Materials

For the Student

    📖 Map of the Revolutionary War

    📖 Revolutionary War: People and Places

    A History of US (Concise Edition), Volume A (Prehistory to 1800) by Joy Hakim

    History Journal

# LEARN
## Activity 1: Valley Forge to Vincennes (Offline)
### Instructions
**Check Your Reading (Chapter 70, pages 329–335)**

Go over Chapter 70 with an adult. Then complete the map activity and the descriptions of the first four people on page 2 of the Revolutionary War: People and Places sheet. Refer to the map of the Revolutionary War online to complete the map activity.

You will complete more activities on the sheet in the next lesson.

### Discuss

Discuss the following two questions with an adult:

- Although no battles were fought at Valley Forge, it is considered a major American triumph. Why?
- What was all the fighting in the West about?

## Use What You Know

Write a letter about Valley Forge in your History Journal:

- Reread the letter from Dr. Albigence Waldo in Chapter 70.
- Imagine you are Dr. Waldo and it's now spring. You have survived the terrible winter.
- Write a letter describing the changes that have taken place in the troops and in your morale.

## Read On

As the war dragged on, it became more and more unpopular in England. But time did not diminish the Americans' belief in their cause. This gave the colonists an advantage over their English cousins. Soon the war in the northern colonies became a stalemate. Sir William Howe resigned. The new British commander shifted his attention to the southern colonies. How would the Patriots react in Georgia and South Carolina? Would Washington get the help he desperately needed from the French?

Read Chapter 71, pages 336–343. Be prepared to explain the roles geography and the French played in Cornwallis's defeat at Yorktown.

## Optional: Beyond the Lesson

Explore the Valley Forge National Historic Park online. The site contains many images of Revolutionary War-era artifacts.

## Activity 2. Optional: Valley Forge *(Online)*

Name _____ Date _____

# Revolutionary War: People and Places

Add the following to the map below: Saratoga, Philadelphia, Valley Forge, and Vincennes.

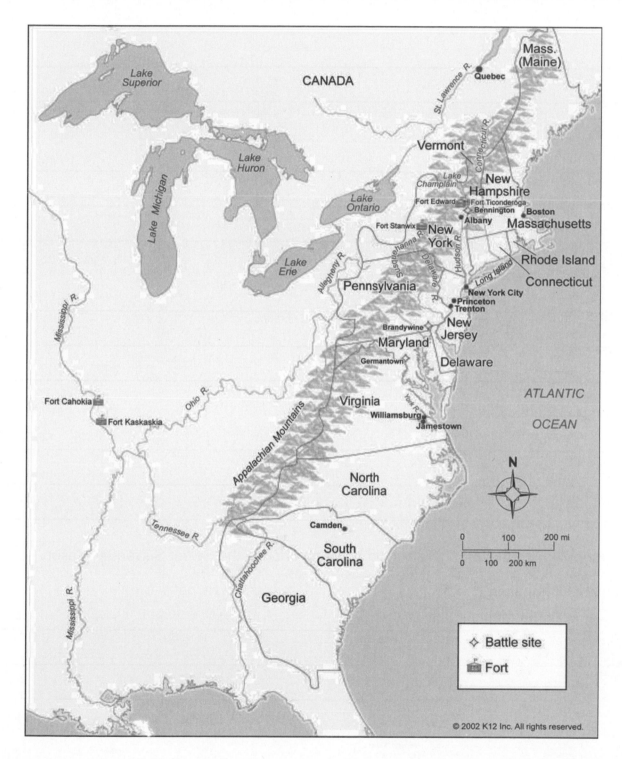

Write a brief description of each person. Include any information you've learned that you believe is important and/or interesting.

1. George Washington

   _____

   _____

   _____

2. Martha Washington

   _____

   _____

   _____

3. Nathanael Greene

   _____

   _____

   _____

4. George Rogers Clark

   _____

   _____

   _____

The descriptions for these people should be written during the Sweet Surrender lesson.

5. Alexander Hamilton

   _____

   _____

   _____

**6.** General Henry Clinton

_____

_____

_____

**7.** Lord Charles Cornwallis

_____

_____

_____

**8.** Comte de Grasse

_____

_____

_____

# Revolutionary War

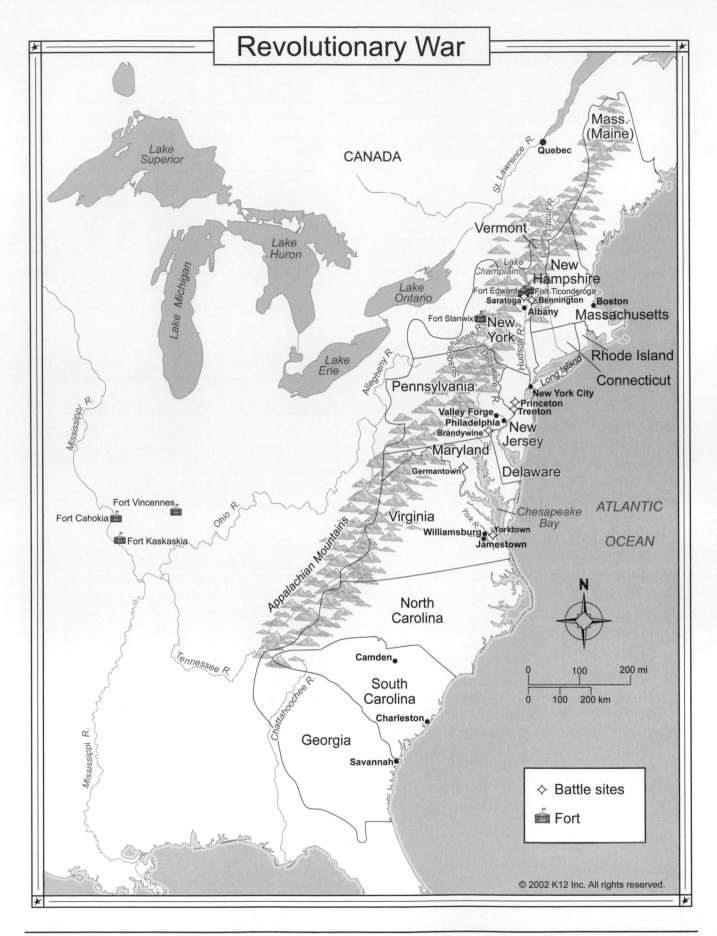

Lake Superior

Lake Huron

Lake Michigan

Lake Ontario

Lake Erie

CANADA

St. Lawrence R.

Quebec

Mass. (Maine)

Vermont

New Hampshire

Lake Champlain

Connecticut R.

Fort Edward    Fort Ticonderoga
Saratoga    Bennington    Boston
Fort Stanwix    Albany    Massachusetts
New York    Rhode Island
Hudson R.    Long Island    Connecticut

Allegheny R.
Susquehanna R.
Delaware R.
Pennsylvania    New York City
Princeton
Trenton
Valley Forge    New
Philadelphia    Jersey
Brandywine
Maryland    Delaware

Germantown

Mississippi R.

Fort Vincennes
Fort Cahokia
Fort Kaskaskia

Ohio R.

Appalachian Mountains

Virginia
York R.    Chesapeake Bay
Williamsburg    Yorktown
Jamestown

ATLANTIC OCEAN

North Carolina

Tennessee R.

Chattahoochee R.

Camden

South Carolina

Charleston

Georgia

Savannah

N

0    100    200 mi
0    100    200 km

◇ Battle sites
🏰 Fort

Mississippi R.

© 2002 K12 Inc. All rights reserved.

# Student Guide
## Lesson 6: Sweet Surrender

With the help of France, the Americans finally backed the British into a corner at Yorktown. The fife and drum played a tune that summed up American victory: "The World Turned Upside Down."

## Lesson Objectives

- Demonstrate mastery of important knowledge and skills taught in previous lessons.
- Locate the following places on a map: Savannah, Charleston, Chesapeake Bay, and Yorktown, and U.S. boundaries in 1783.
- Identify Cornwallis as the leader of the British forces and Alexander Hamilton as aide to George Washington.
- Explain the role of geography and the French in Cornwallis's defeat at Yorktown.
- Analyze art of the Revolution to determine the values it promotes.
- Explain the significance of the Declaration of Independence in unifying people for the war effort.
- Describe the roles of women during the Revolution, including maintaining farms and businesses, assisting in the war effort, fighting, and being politically vocal.
- Define *Hessian* and *mercenary*.
- Identify Sir William Howe as the commander in charge of all the British forces in America.
- Describe the difficulties George Washington faced as commander of the Continental Army, including a small, unstable army, lack of supplies, and need to use retreat as a way to save the army.
- Explain the significance of the battles of Trenton and Saratoga (one boosted American morale; the other was a turning point in the war).
- Locate the following places on a map: Saratoga, Philadelphia, Valley Forge, and Vincennes.
- Identify Martha Washington as providing moral support and Nathaniel Greene and George Rogers Clark as significant military leaders of the Revolution.
- Describe conditions at Valley Forge and summarize the significance of the winter there.
- Explain the reasons for the warfare on the frontier and the effect of the Revolution on Native Americans.

---

# PREPARE

Approximate lesson time is 60 minutes.

## Materials

For the Student

    📖 Map of the Revolutionary War

    A History of US (Concise Edition), Volume A (Prehistory to 1800) by Joy Hakim

    History Journal

    📖 The American Revolution Assessment Sheet

---

# LEARN
## Activity 1: The World Turned Upside Down (Offline)
### Instructions
**Check Your Reading (Chapter 71, pages 336–343)**

Refer to the Revolutionary War map to add these places to the map on page 1 of the Revolutionary War: People and Places sheet:

- Savannah
- Charleston
- Chesapeake Bay
- Yorktown

Show the boundaries of the United States in 1783 using boundary lines or shading. (Use the map of North America in 1783 in Chapter 71 as a reference.)

Now add a description for each of the following people on the same sheet:

- Alexander Hamilton
- General Henry Clinton
- Lord Charles Cornwallis
- Comte de Grasse

### Discuss

1. How did the geography at Yorktown help the Americans defeat the British?
2. What role did the French play in the British defeat at Yorktown?
3. Why do you think the tune "The World Turned Upside Down" was a fitting way to end the Revolution?

### Analyze Art of the Revolution

Go back to the lesson online and analyze a painting about the Revolutionary War. Discuss these questions with an adult:

1.  In *The Spirit of '76,* by Archibald Willard, two men and a boy play music while leading a parade of soldiers. Did the artist paint a realistic and orderly scene or an emotional scene to get you to experience what he's showing in the painting? What details tell you that?
2.  Do you think the artist valued freedom and liberty? Why or why not?
3.  Why do you think the artist included a flag in the painting? What is the flag a symbol of? How do you feel when you look at your country's flag?
4.  Do you think the artist created a painting to influence the way people feel? If so, do you think he succeeded? How did he do this?

# ASSESS

## Mid-Unit Assessment: The American Revolution (*Offline*)

You will complete an offline Mid-Unit Assessment covering the main goals for Lessons 4, 5, and 6. An adult will score the assessment and enter the results online.

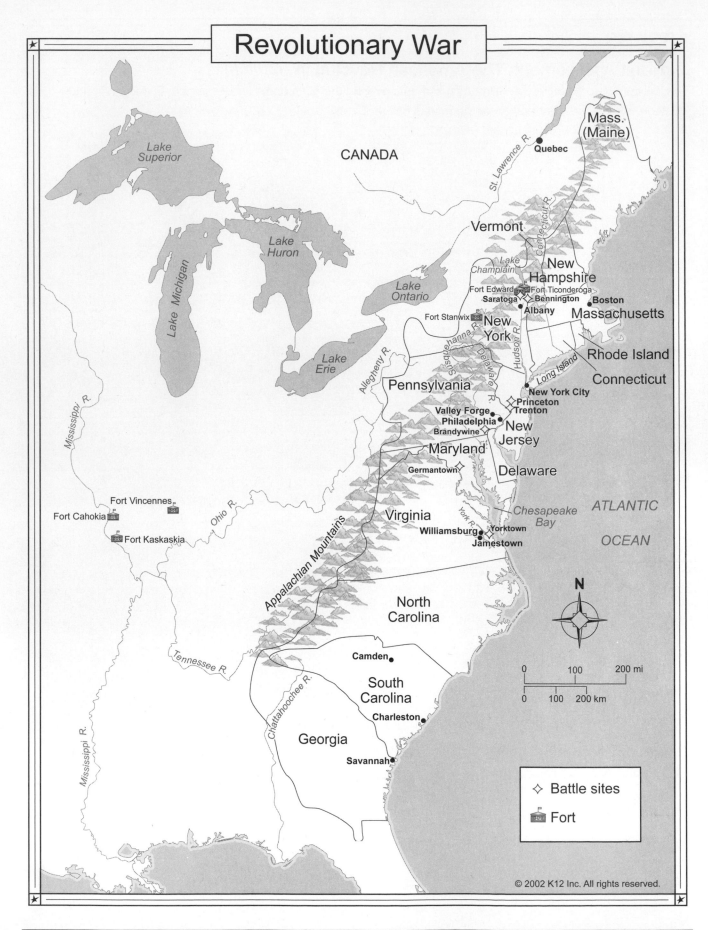

# Revolutionary War

CANADA

Lake Superior

Lake Michigan

Lake Huron

Lake Erie

Lake Ontario

St. Lawrence R.

Quebec

Mass. (Maine)

Vermont

Lake Champlain

Connecticut R.

New Hampshire

Fort Edward · Fort Ticonderoga
Saratoga ◇ · Bennington
Fort Stanwix

Albany

Boston

Massachusetts

New York

Susquehanna R.

Hudson R.

Delaware R.

Rhode Island

Connecticut

Long Island

New York City
Princeton ◇
Trenton

Allegheny R.

Pennsylvania

Valley Forge ·
Philadelphia · Brandywine ◇

New Jersey

Mississippi R.

Maryland

Germantown ◇

Delaware

Fort Vincennes

Ohio R.

Fort Cahokia

Fort Kaskaskia

Virginia

Williamsburg · ◇ Yorktown
Jamestown

York R.

Chesapeake Bay

ATLANTIC

OCEAN

Tennessee R.

North Carolina

N

Camden ·

South Carolina

Charleston ·

Chattahoochee R.

Georgia

Savannah ·

0        100        200 mi
0    100    200 km

◇ Battle sites

🏰 Fort

Appalachian Mountains

Mississippi R.

Name                                                                Date

# Mid-Unit Assessment

1. What is a mercenary?

   (A) a person hired to obtain supplies for an army

   (B) a soldier hired to fight for another country

   (C) a general hired to train foreign troops

   (D) a commander in charge of an entire force

2. What group of people did Washington surprise and capture after crossing the Delaware?

   (A) Frenchmen

   (B) Spaniards

   (C) Hessians

   (D) British redcoats

3. The victory in which battle convinced the French to join the war on the side of the Americans?

   (A) Saratoga

   (B) Trenton

   (C) Yorktown

   (D) Valley Forge

4. What strategy did Washington use in the early part of the war?

   (A) He attacked the enemy regardless of losses to his army.

   (B) He used Native American allies to attack the French.

   (C) He used his navy to blockade English ports in the West Indies.

   (D) He retreated whenever necessary to save his army.

5. The battle of Trenton was an important battle for the Americans because _____ .

Ⓐ their victory raised morale among the colonists

Ⓑ the British victory convinced the French to join the war

Ⓒ the colonists captured Howe's forces in New York

Ⓓ their defeat convinced the French to help them

6. What effect did the Revolutionary War have on Native Americans?

Ⓐ It had no effect on Native Americans.

Ⓑ Native Americans lost a lot of land.

Ⓒ Native Americans gained lands taken by the French.

Ⓓ British soldiers forced Native Americans onto reservations.

7. Which of these statements is true about Valley Forge?

Ⓐ During the winter the Americans defeated a large British army.

Ⓑ The British had to retreat from Valley Forge before an advancing Continental Army.

Ⓒ After Valley Forge the Continental Army was better trained, with a new spirit of unity.

Ⓓ French military commanders used Valley Forge as a base for raids into the frontier.

8. Match each person on the left with the description of the person on the right.

_____ William Howe

_____ Martha Washington

_____ Nathanael Greene

_____ George Rogers Clark

_____ Alexander Hamilton

_____ Lord Cornwallis

A. American colonel and aide to Washington who captured a key British earth fortress at Yorktown

B. Quartermaster general of the Continental Army; brought caches of food and supplies to Valley Forge and led troops in the South

C. Commander of all British forces in America until 1778

D. Naval hero who defeated the British ship Serapis and said, "I have not yet begun to fight."

E. Commander of British troops in the South; lost the battle at Yorktown

F. Frontiersman who fought the British and their Indian allies in the Ohio Valley

G. General's wife who helped boost morale at Valley Forge

*(6 points—one for each difficulty included in the answer)*

**9.** In complete sentences, describe the difficulties Washington faced as commander of the Continental Army.

_____

_____

_____

_____

_____

_____

**10.** Label the following locations on the map: Savannah, Charleston, Chesapeake Bay, Yorktown, Saratoga, Philadelphia, Valley Forge, and Vincennes. (8 points—one for each location correctly labeled on the map)

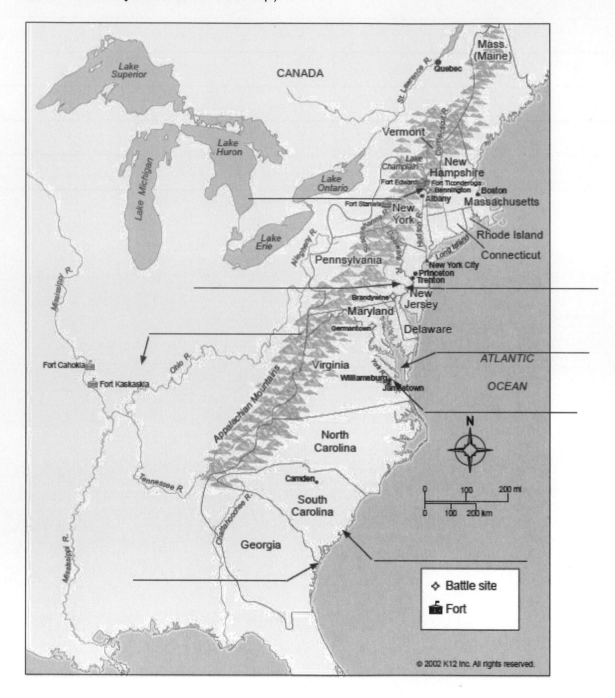

# *Student Guide*
## Lesson 7: (Optional) What Did It All Mean?

From the signing of the Declaration to the victory at Yorktown, Americans turned their dreams of liberty into a new nation. The American Revolution was a defining period in American history that brought about many changes.

### Lesson Objectives
- Summarize the key events and ideas of the Revolution.
- Analyze the changes that the Revolution brought about.

# PREPARE

Approximate lesson time is 60 minutes.

### Materials

For the Student

🖥 Revolutionary Changes

A History of US (Concise Edition), Volume A (Prehistory to 1800) by Joy Hakim

History Journal

# LEARN
## Activity 1. Optional: Revolutionary Changes *(Offline)*
### Instructions
### Use What You Know

Revolutionary Changes

On the Revolutionary Changes sheet, examine the list of changes that came about as a result of the Revolution. Decide whether each change supported or conflicted with the values of the Revolution.

Liberty! The American Revolution

Go back online to explore the PBS website *Liberty! The American Revolution.* This site has many interesting sections. You may be especially interested in these two:

- The Road to Revolution Game
- Chronicles of the Revolution

Name _____ Date _____

## Revolutionary Changes

Read the following list of changes that came about as a result of the American Revolution. For each change, indicate whether you believe the change supported or conflicted with the values of the Revolution.

1. Men no longer tipped their hats to those of a higher class.

   SUPPORTED or CONFLICTED

2. A number of planters and others freed their slaves.

   SUPPORTED or CONFLICTED

3. George Washington resigned his commission in the army and returned to being a farmer.

   SUPPORTED or CONFLICTED

4. Academies for women were established.

   SUPPORTED or CONFLICTED

5. Men stopped wearing wigs and powdering their hair in the English fashion.

   SUPPORTED or CONFLICTED

6. About 100,000 Loyalists left the country for their own physical or political security.

   SUPPORTED or CONFLICTED

7. Laws requiring a man to leave his entire estate to his eldest son and not split it up were taken off the books.

   SUPPORTED or CONFLICTED

8. The first representative government for a large nation in modern history was formed.

   SUPPORTED or CONFLICTED

Merriam-Webster's Collegiate Dictionary defines revolution as "a sudden, radical, or complete change." Many historians argue that the American Revolution was really a war for independence, rather than a revolution. What do you think?

# *Student Guide*
## Lesson 8: Unit Review

You've completed Unit 6, The American Revolution. It's time to review what you've learned. You'll take the unit assessment in the next lesson.

### Lesson Objectives

- Demonstrate mastery of important knowledge and skills taught in previous lessons.
- Make quilt squares that represent the major events, people, and ideas from the American Revolution.

---

# PREPARE

Approximate lesson time is 60 minutes.

### Materials

    For the Student

        A History of US (Concise Edition), Volume A (Prehistory to 1800) by Joy Hakim

        History Journal

---

# LEARN
## Activity 1: A Look Back *(Offline)*
### Instructions
### History Journal Review

Review the unit by going through your History Journal. You should:

- Look at worksheets you have completed for this unit.
- Review unit vocabulary words.
- Read through any writing assignments you did during the unit.
- Review the two assessments you took.

### Online Review

Go online and use the following to review this unit:

- The Big Picture
- Flash Cards
- Time Line
- *Liberty! The American Revolution*
- Map of Revolutionary War

---

**Beyond the Lesson**

Create squares for a quilt that symbolizes the major events, people, and ideas from the American Revolution.

## Activity 2: Revolutionary Quilt *(Offline)*

# *Student Guide*
## Lesson 9: Unit Assessment

You've finished this unit! Take the Unit Assessment. Then look at today's reading assignment.

### Lesson Objectives
- Recognize John Adams's role in declaring independence as one of early and persistent support.
- Explain the significance of the Declaration of Independence in unifying people for the war effort.
- Summarize the dilemma many blacks faced in taking sides during the Revolution.
- Describe the roles of blacks on both sides of the conflict.
- Identify individuals who came from Europe to aid the American cause, including the Marquis de Lafayette, Baron Friedrich von Steuben, and Haym Salomon.
- Define *Hessian* and *mercenary.*
- Explain the significance of the battles of Trenton and Saratoga (one boosted American morale; the other was a turning point in the war).
- Identify Martha Washington as providing moral support and Nathaniel Greene and George Rogers Clark as significant military leaders of the Revolution.
- Describe conditions at Valley Forge and summarize the significance of the winter there.
- Explain the reasons for the warfare on the frontier and the effect of the Revolution on Native Americans.
- Identify Cornwallis as the leader of the British forces and Alexander Hamilton as aide to George Washington.
- Explain the role of geography and the French in Cornwallis's defeat at Yorktown.
- Identify George Washington as providing example, dignity and determination to his army.
- Identify Abigail Adams as a delegate's wife who wrote letters to her husband about the unequal treatment of women and blacks.

---

# PREPARE

Approximate lesson time is 60 minutes.

## Materials

For the Student

    📖 The American Revolution Assessment Sheet

    A History of US (Concise Edition), Volume A (Prehistory to 1800) by Joy Hakim

    History Journal

# ASSESS

## Unit Assessment: The American Revolution (*Offline*)

Complete the offline Unit Assessment. Your Learning Coach will score it and enter the results online.

# LEARN

## Activity 1: Chapters 72 and 73 (*Offline*)

### Instructions

After they had won their independence, American citizens saw themselves more as a collection of 13 states than as one strong nation. In fact, it might have been more accurate to call them the "Disunited States of America."

You will learn about successes and failures in the first attempt to form a government. You will also learn how those successes and failures set the stage for the creation of a strong U.S. Constitution.

Read Chapter 72, pages 344–346, and Chapter 73, pages 347–349. Be prepared to discuss these concepts:

- constitutional convention
- separation of powers
- bill of rights
- freedom of religion
- Articles of Confederation

Name                                    Date

# Unit Assessment

1. How did John Adams help persuade the delegates to sign the Declaration of Independence?

    (A) He told the delegates the French would help if they signed it.

    (B) He threatened delegates who were opposed to independence.

    (C) He never gave up and spoke convincingly about independence.

    (D) He wrote much of the document with Thomas Jefferson.

2. How did the Declaration of Independence affect most colonists?

    (A) They were afraid that each state would fight Britain independently.

    (B) They were sad and felt bad for leaving the mother country.

    (C) They felt disappointed with the actions of the delegates.

    (D) They were proud and felt like a part of a larger group.

3. Britain encouraged slaves to leave their American owners and help Britain by promising them _____ .

    (A) freedom

    (B) voting rights

    (C) land

    (D) a salary

4. Why did the Continental Army refuse to enlist blacks in the early years of the war?

    (A) Officers were concerned they would desert and go over to the British forces.

    (B) Many whites feared a slave uprising if blacks had guns.

    (C) The army could not afford to pay any more soldiers' salaries.

    (D) The army only allowed people born in Britain or the colonies to enlist.

5. What kind of military men did the British hire to fight against the colonists in America? What country were they from?

   (A) mercenaries; Russia

   (B) mercenaries; Germany

   (C) sailors; Spain

   (D) cavalry; Portugal

6. The French decided to join the war on the side of the colonists after the American victory in which battle?

   (A) Lexington

   (B) Yorktown

   (C) Saratoga

   (D) Charleston

7. What strategy was George Washington forced to use during the early part of the war?

   (A) Attack the enemy regardless of losses to his army.

   (B) Always fight in the traditional style of European armies.

   (C) Hire Spanish mercenaries to attack British forts in Ohio.

   (D) Retreat whenever necessary to reduce losses to his army.

8. What was an important outcome of the battle of Trenton?

   (A) The American army lost thousands of soldiers.

   (B) The American victory boosted morale among the colonists.

   (C) The British defeat signaled the end of the Revolution.

   (D) Sir William Howe resigned as commander of British forces in America.

9. Which of these statements about Native Americans and the American Revolution is true?

   (A) Britain avoided any agreements with Native Americans.

   (B) Regardless of which side they chose, Native Americans lost land during the war.

   (C) The Continental Congress promised to give western lands to Native Americans.

   (D) Most Native Americans allied themselves with the Americans and fought against Britain.

10. What was the importance of Valley Forge to the Americans in the Revolutionary War?

   (A) After Valley Forge, the American army was stronger, prouder, and better trained.

   (B) The French army was able to use Valley Forge as a base for raids into Canada.

   (C) The British were not able to defeat the Americans and so withdrew from Philadelphia.

   (D) During the winter at Valley Forge, American forces were able to retake New York.

11. Which of these statements about the Revolutionary War on the frontier is true?

   (A) American frontiersmen used unconventional tactics to frustrate the British.

   (B) The French captured three forts from George Rogers Clark.

   (C) Patrick Henry sent George Rogers Clark to take the Ohio Valley from the French.

   (D) British forces were unable to move back into the Ohio Valley.

(6 points)

12. Match each person on the left with the description on the right. There is one extra description on the right that does not match any of the people on the left.

_____ Baron Friedrich von Steuben

_____ Alexander Hamilton

_____ Lord Cornwallis

_____ Abigail Adams

_____ Marquis de Lafayette

_____ Martha Washington

A. General's wife who helped boost morale at Valley Forge

B. Commander of British troops in the South who lost the battle at Yorktown

C. Former Prussian captain who turned a disorderly group of American recruits into skilled soldiers

D. Frontiersman who fought the British and their Indian allies in the Ohio Valley

E. Delegate's wife who wrote letters to her husband about the unequal treatment of women and blacks

F. Frenchman who became a general on George Washington's staff and Washington's lifelong friend

G. Colonial officer on Washington's staff who captured a British fort during the battle at Yorktown

(4 points)

13. Describe the ways in which George Washington inspired the Continental Army and served as an example for his soldiers to follow.

_____

_____

_____

_____

14. What role did the French play in the British defeat at Yorktown?

_____

_____

_____

_____

# Student Guide
## Lesson 1: Confederation and Constitutions

The government that came to power in 1789 was an experiment, established by the first enduring written constitution in history. Success and failure under the Articles of Confederation set the stage for a new plan of government. Hard work, compromise, and the genius of men like James Madison and Alexander Hamilton made the Constitution a reality.

After they won their independence, American citizens saw themselves more as a collection of 13 states than as one strong nation. Fortunately, each state had written its own state constitution. Unfortunately, people were so wary of a strong national government that they created a weak one. The lessons learned from these two actions paved the way for the creation of the U.S. Constitution.

### Lesson Objectives
- Explain the need for and significance of state constitutions during the Revolution.
- Define *separation of powers* as the division of political power among branches of government.
- Identify the Articles of Confederation as the first government of the United States and describe its weaknesses, including the lack of an executive and of taxing power.
- Identify traditional English freedoms, such as trial by jury, guaranteed in state constitutions' bills of rights, and identify freedom of religion as a new freedom in state constitutions.

# PREPARE

Approximate lesson time is 60 minutes.

### Materials
For the Student

    🖳 Strong Constitutions, Weak Confederation

    A History of US (Concise Edition), Volume A (Prehistory to 1800) by Joy Hakim

    History Journal

# LEARN
## Activity 1: The Disunited States of America *(Offline)*
### Instructions
**Check Your Reading (Chapter 72, pages 344–346, and Chapter 73, pages 347–349)**

- Print the Strong Constitutions, Weak Confederation sheet and fill out as much as you can from memory.
- Review Chapters 72 and 73.
- Fill in any missing answers on the Strong Constitutions, Weak Confederation sheet, and check all your answers against the book. When you think you've got them all right, check your answers with an adult.

**Use What You Know**

Think about what you have read and answer the following questions in your History Journal. Discuss your answers with an adult.

1. Why was it important that each state write a constitution? How was that helpful for the future?
2. What document formed the first government of the newly independent American states? Why was it so weak? What were its two major weaknesses? How was its weakness helpful for the future?

**Assessment**

There is no assessment in this lesson.

**Read On**

Read Chapter 74, pages 350–353. Be prepared to discuss the reasons for the Northwest Ordinance and to describe its provisions.

Vocabulary

You'll see these terms as you read. Write a brief definition for each term in your History Journal.

- ordinance
- involuntary servitude

**Optional: Beyond the Lesson**

Go online to learn about your state's origins and constitution.

# Activity 2. Optional: Your State's Constitution *(Online)*

Name _____     Date _____

## Strong Constitutions, Weak Confederation

Fill in the blanks to answer these questions with choices from the answer box on page 3.

1. The colonists knew that they had to come up with a new form of government to replace the British after the war was over. The Continental Congress suggested that each state

   write a _____ .

2. This drawing represents the "tree of government." Label the three branches of this tree. In each label, write a word that describes one branch. At the bottom of the picture, write a caption that describes all three branches of government.

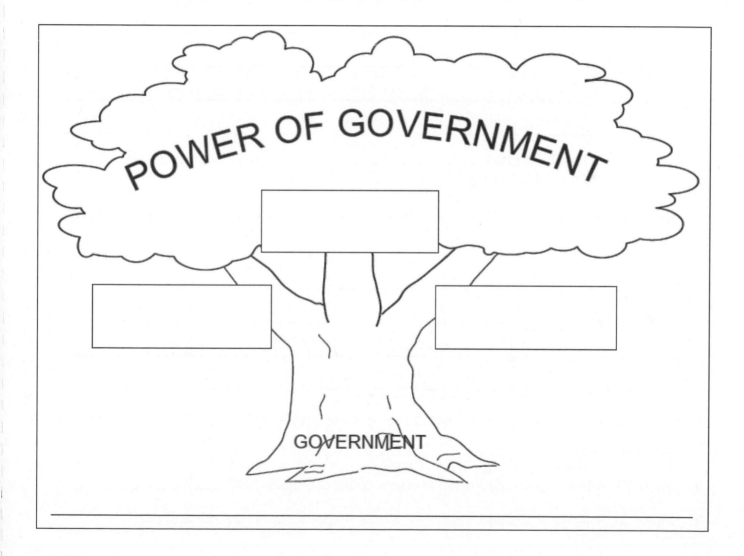

POWER OF GOVERNMENT

GOVERNMENT

3. In 1780, Massachusetts was the first state to use a particular process to write and adopt its constitution. Identify and describe that process. The name of the process is in the answer box—you have to come up with the description.

_____

_____

_____

4. Identify six things that states discussed including in their constitutions.

_____

_____

_____

_____

5. Every state constitution had a _____. Virginia's, written by George Mason, was a model for many others.

6. Identify five English rights Americans were determined to have in their state constitutions.

_____

_____

_____

_____

_____

7. The Virginia constitution went beyond the rights of Englishmen and added an extra, new

right. What was it? _____

8. Under the Articles of Confederation, whom could Congress tax? _____

9. Under the Articles of Confederation, who was responsible for the printing of money?

_____

10. What was the basic problem with the Articles of Confederation? _____

_____

## Bonus Question

The answer to this question is not in the answer box. On November 5, 1781, who became the first president of the newly independent American states?

| **Answer Box** |
|---|
| *Alert! One of these answers is used twice!* |
| • Constitution |
| • Separation of powers |
| • Freedom of religion |
| • Executive (governor) |
| • Bill of Rights |
| • Constitutional Convention |
| • Freedom of speech and of the press |
| • It was too weak to do a good job. |
| • Judicial (courts) |
| • Free education |
| • The right of the majority to change the government |
| • The right of citizens not to be taxed without their consent or that of their representatives |
| • Nobody |
| • Free elections |
| • Each state and the Congress |
| • Government power derived from the people |
| • The right to a trial by jury |
| • Slavery |
| • Voting rights |
| • Protection against unreasonable arrest |
| • Legislative (assembly) |

# Student Guide
## Lesson 2: The Northwest Ordinance

The greatest act of the government under the Articles of Confederation was the passage of the Northwest Ordinance in 1787. This law set the rules for the settlement of the Northwest Territory—the western land claims that Virginia and other states gave up. It included a bill of rights for the settlers. It also provided for the creation of public schools. It established a way for settlements to organize as states and join the rest of the nation.

## Lesson Objectives
- Review a map of the new nation and identify the western lands under dispute.
- Summarize the reasons for and major provisions of the Northwest Ordinance.
- Explain the importance of the Northwest Ordinance in terms of future territories and the precedents it set for education and slavery.

---

# PREPARE

Approximate lesson time is 60 minutes.

## Materials
For the Student

📖 The Northwest Ordinance

A History of US (Concise Edition), Volume A (Prehistory to 1800) by Joy Hakim

History Journal

---

# LEARN
## Activity 1: Thirteen States and More to Come (Offline)
### Instructions
Check Your Reading (Chapter 74, pages 350–353)

Review Chapter 74 by completing the Northwest Ordinance sheet. Check your answers with an adult.

### Discuss

1. One of the "firsts" in world history was the American plan in the Northwest Ordinance to provide a means for territories to join the Union as states on an equal footing with the other states. Why was this a "first"? Why was it important?
2. Why did Americans feel that it was important to require townships to set aside land for public schools and for the territories to encourage education?

### Assessment

There is no assessment in this lesson.

---

**Read On**

Thomas Jefferson was fascinated with the Northwest Territory. He valued education and political power for all citizens. Jefferson was a thinker who promoted several important ideas in American government, including the separation of church and state.

Read Chapter 75, pages 354–357. Be prepared to discuss how hard it is to get people to accept new ideas.

Name _____     Date _____

## The Northwest Ordinance

You'll find the answers to these questions in Chapter 74. Write your answers in the spaces provided.

1. What happened to Native Americans when Great Britain lost control of the colonies?

   _____

   _____

   _____

2. Five states and a part of a sixth state would eventually form from the Northwest Territory. What are those states? _____

   _____

3. The Confederation Congress passed the Northwest Ordinance in 1787. Under what government did the Confederation Congress exist? _____

4. The new states had until recently been British colonies. How did their memory of that experience affect their view of the western lands? _____

   _____

   _____

   _____

5. What ordinance established a system for dividing land into townships?

   _____

6. What did this system also allow townships to do? _____

   _____

7. The Northwest Ordinance guaranteed three rights for the settlers of the Northwest Territory. What were they? _____

   _____

8. The Northwest Ordinance had a number of "firsts." Two in particular were important to the course of American history. One dealt with slavery and another with education. Describe how these two issues were provided for in the Northwest Territory.

_____

_____

_____

_____

9. What provision did the Northwest Ordinance have for the Indians? Do you think it was

enforced? Give a reason for what you think. _____

_____

_____

10. From Settlement to State

How does a region go from having almost no settlers to becoming a state? The Northwest Ordinance had a plan.

Put the events listed here in correct sequence to describe how settlements could evolve into states. Write the numbers 1 through 4 in the spaces provided with 1 being the earliest event and 4 being the latest.

The chapter does not explicitly describe the order. Use what you have learned and what makes sense to sequence these events in the correct order.

_____ Townships organize into a territory.

_____ Settlers start farms, towns, and businesses.

_____ When territories get a large enough population, they can apply for statehood.

_____ Settlements organize into a township.

# Student Guide
## Lesson 3: Thomas Jefferson: A Man for All Time

You know Thomas Jefferson as the author of the Declaration of Independence. He was also secretary of state, vice president, and president of the United States. He was an architect, a violinist, a mathematician, an inventor, an experimental farmer, and a natural scientist. He spoke six languages. And there is more.

### Lesson Objectives

- Demonstrate knowledge gained in previous lessons.
- Describe Thomas Jefferson as accomplished in areas including philosophy, government, arts, and sciences.
- Use the Internet to gain information on Thomas Jefferson.
- Explain the need for and significance of state constitutions during the Revolution.
- Define *separation of powers* as the division of political power among branches of government.
- Identify the Articles of Confederation as the first government of the United States and describe its weaknesses, including the lack of an executive and of taxing power.
- Review a map of the new nation and identify the western lands under dispute.
- Explain the importance of the Northwest Ordinance in terms of future territories and the precedents it set for education and slavery.
- Identify traditional English freedoms, such as trial by jury, guaranteed in state constitutions' bills of rights, and identify freedom of religion as a new freedom in state constitutions.

---

# PREPARE

Approximate lesson time is 60 minutes.

### Materials

For the Student

    A History of US (Concise Edition), Volume A (Prehistory to 1800) by Joy Hakim

    map, U.S.

    History Journal

    ⬚ Thomas Jefferson: A Man for All Time Assessment Sheet

---

# LEARN
## Activity 1: The Renaissance Man of Monticello *(Offline)*
### Instructions
Check Your Reading (Chapter 75, pages 354–357)

In your History Journal, write a paragraph expressing your thoughts about Thomas Jefferson and his accomplishments.

---

## Use What You Know

Go online and visit the Monticello website. You may take a quiz on Thomas Jefferson or go on a scavenger hunt about his life. If you finish the quiz, print the Congratulations screen!

## Look Back

- Review Lessons 1-3 of Unit 7 (Chapters 72, 73, 74, and 75).
- In your History Journal, look at the activity sheets you completed for these lessons. Review your vocabulary words. If you completed any writing assignments, read them. Don't rush through; take your time. Your History Journal is a great resource for lesson reviews.
- Go online and review the First U.S. Government flash cards.

## Assessment

Take the assessment.

## Read On

Do you remember all the problems the country was having with its government under the Articles of Confederation? James Madison couldn't stop thinking about them. When delegates met in Philadelphia in the hot summer of 1787, he was ready to make a plan for a whole new government. Why were delegates gathering that summer? What ideas did they have for solving their problems? And why did they decide to keep everything they did a secret?

Read Chapter 76, pages 358–363. Be prepared to discuss James Madison's background and talents and the importance of his work before and during the convention.

Vocabulary

As you read, write a brief definition for each of these terms in your History Journal.

- Virginia Plan
- Framers

# ASSESS

## Mid-Unit Assessment: Thomas Jefferson: A Man for All Time (*Offline*)

You will complete an offline Mid-Unit Assessment covering the main goals for Lessons 1, 2, and 3. An adult will score the assessment and enter the results online.

Name _____ Date _____

## Mid-Unit Assessment

1. Why did each of the 13 states write a constitution soon after independence was declared?

   _____

   _____

   _____

2. Define *separation of powers*.

   _____

   _____

3. What freedom did Virginia include in its constitution that had not been a right under British government?

   _____

4. What were the Articles of Confederation?

   _____

   _____

5. Which letter on the map on the next page indicates the region known as the Northwest Territory? _____

6. Name three things the Northwest Ordinance provided for or prohibited in the Northwest Territory.

   _____

   _____

   _____

7. Why is Thomas Jefferson considered an accomplished man, or a Renaissance man?

   _____

   _____

   _____

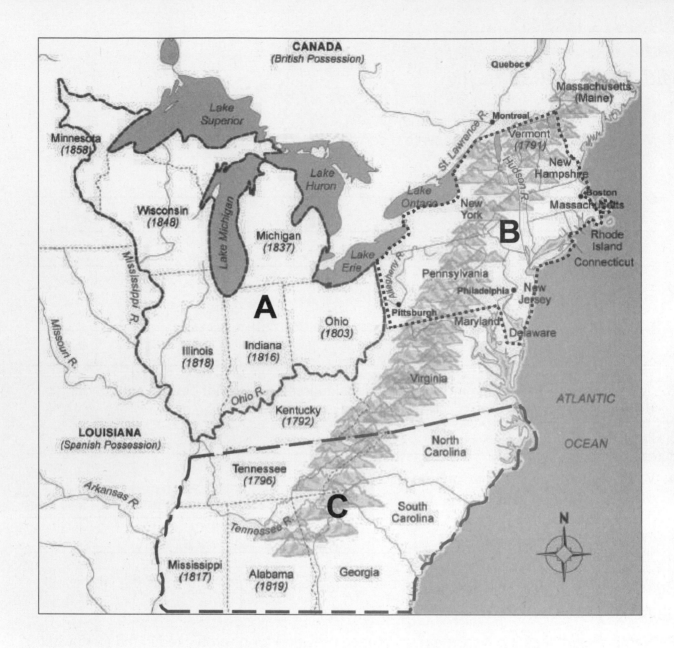

# Student Guide
## Lesson 4: James Madison and a Philadelphia Summer

James Madison thought the Articles of Confederation had to be abandoned and a new constitution written to take their place. When the Constitutional Convention met in Philadelphia, he came with a plan. As they worked throughout a sweltering summer, the delegates kept their discussions secret. What came out of those meetings was the U.S. Constitution.

### Lesson Objectives

- Identify James Madison as the man given the title "Father of the Constitution."
- Summarize the background and talent James Madison brought to the Constitutional Convention, including scholarship and willingness to work hard.
- Explain that the reason for calling the convention in Philadelphia was the need to revise the Articles of Confederation or write a new Constitution.
- Recognize the arguments for and against keeping the convention debates a secret.

# PREPARE

Approximate lesson time is 60 minutes.

### Materials

For the Student

🖥 Convention Secrecy

A History of US (Concise Edition), Volume A (Prehistory to 1800) by Joy Hakim

History Journal

# LEARN
## Activity 1: Summer in Philadelphia (Offline)
### Instructions
**Check Your Reading (Chapter 76, pages 358–363)**

Review Chapter 76 by writing the answers to these questions in complete sentences in your History Journal.

1. What talents did James Madison bring to the Constitutional Convention?
2. How did Thomas Jefferson, Madison's good friend, help him at the Constitutional Convention?
3. Based on what you know about the Articles of Confederation, why do you think James Madison wanted to abandon them?
4. Why did the Framers adopt a secrecy rule?
5. Why has James Madison been called "the Father of the Constitution"?

**Use What You Know**

## Use What You Know

Complete the Convention Secrecy sheet on the pros and cons of keeping the convention a secret. Then decide what you think. Explain to an adult why you believe the convention meetings should or should not have been kept secret.

## Read On

Many issues divided delegates, but the most explosive one was political power. Some delegates wanted strong state governments; others wanted a strong national government. Out of the debate came a compromise—a federal system in which governments share power.

Another conflict over power erupted when big and little states battled over representation. Roger Sherman settled the matter with a compromise.

Read Chapter 77, pages 364–369.

Vocabulary

You'll see these terms as you read. Write a brief definition for each term in your History Journal.

- confederation
- federation
- Virginia Plan
- New Jersey Plan
- Connecticut Compromise

Name _____     Date _____

## Convention Secrecy

Write the reasons for keeping the Constitutional Convention a secret (pros) on one side of the balance scale, and the reasons it should not be kept secret (cons) on the other side.

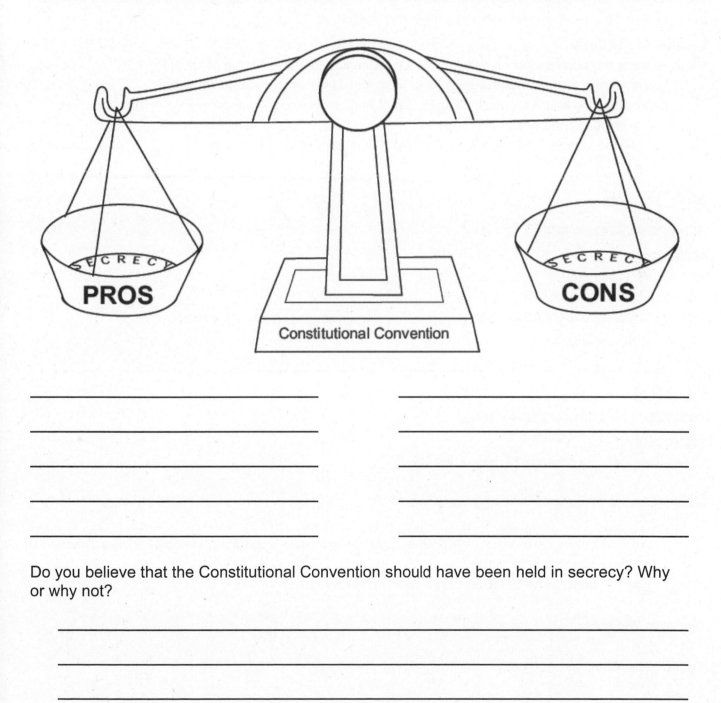

**PROS**          Constitutional Convention          **CONS**

_____          _____

_____          _____

_____          _____

_____          _____

Do you believe that the Constitutional Convention should have been held in secrecy? Why or why not?

_____

_____

_____

_____

# Student Guide
## Lesson 5: An Important Compromise

The delegates at the Constitutional Convention were divided over many things, but power was the most explosive. They had to reach a compromise over representation. Should each state have one vote in the legislature as it did under the Articles of Confederation? Or should the states with more people have more votes? Roger Sherman came up with a solution to the problem.

### Lesson Objectives
- Analyze a political cartoon to gain information on the positions taken at the convention.
- Identify Roger Sherman as the delegate who proposed the compromise we use today.
- Summarize the issues on which the delegates to the Constitutional Convention were divided, including representation and slavery.
- Explain the Virginia Plan and the New Jersey Plan in terms of representation.

# PREPARE

Approximate lesson time is 60 minutes.

### Materials
For the Student

    ⌨ Compromise

    A History of US (Concise Edition), Volume A (Prehistory to 1800) by Joy Hakim

    History Journal

# LEARN
## Activity 1: Compromise (Offline)
### Instructions
Check Your Reading (Chapter 77, pages 364–369)

Review Chapter 77 using the following questions.

1. What was the issue involved in the debate between small and large states? How did the New Jersey and Virginia plans reflect this?
2. How did compromise settle the debate over representation?

Use What You Know

Complete the Compromise sheet.

Read On

The powerful words "We the People" began the Constitution. But exactly whom did those words include? Did they include women, blacks, and Native Americans? Americans are still working toward this ideal.

Read Chapter 78, pages 370–374. Think about the following questions for discussion as you read.

1. What is the basic difference between the Declaration of Independence and the Constitution?
2. What is the purpose of the Preamble?
3. On what issues did the Framers have to make compromises in order to complete the Constitution?
4. Do you think the Framers of the Constitution meant all the people when they wrote the words "We the People"?

Name _____          Date _____

## Compromise

Fill in the chart with information about the Virginia and New Jersey Plans and the Great Compromise.

| Virginia Plan |
|---|
| _____ |
| _____ |
| _____ |
| _____ |
| _____ |
| _____ |
| _____ |

| New Jersey Plan |
|---|
| _____ |
| _____ |
| _____ |
| _____ |
| _____ |
| _____ |
| _____ |

| Great Compromise |
|---|
| _____ |
| _____ |
| _____ |
| _____ |
| _____ |
| _____ |

# Student Guide
## Lesson 6: We the People

"We the People..." begins the Preamble to the Constitution—the document written to put the ideals of the people of this new country into practice. But just who are "the people"? And what were their ideals for government?

### Lesson Objectives

- State the six purposes of the Constitution found in the Preamble.
- Distinguish between the Declaration of Independence and the Constitution.
- Recognize the importance of compromise in writing the Constitution.
- Give concrete examples of the Preamble in practice today.

---

# PREPARE

Approximate lesson time is 60 minutes.

### Materials

For the Student

🖳 Understanding the Preamble

A History of US (Concise Edition), Volume A (Prehistory to 1800) by Joy Hakim

History Journal

---

# LEARN
## Activity 1: Introducing the Constitution (Offline)
### Instructions
#### 1. Check Your Reading (Chapter 78, pages 370–374)

Say the words "We the People . . .", the first three words of the Constitution, aloud. Think about what the words mean. Now, write a paragraph in your History Journal describing your reaction to these words. Discuss your paragraph with an adult.

Answer the following questions in your History Journal to review Chapter 78.

1. What is the basic difference between the Declaration of Independence and the Constitution?
2. What is the purpose of the Preamble?
3. On what issues did the Framers have to make compromises in order to complete the Constitution?
4. Do you think the Framers of the Constitution meant all the people when they wrote the words "We the People"?

---

## 2. Use What You Know

Complete the Understanding the Preamble sheet. First identify the six goals stated in the Preamble. Then, for each goal, redefine the goal in your own words and provide an example of that goal in practice today. A current newspaper may be useful for finding examples.

## 3. Read On

Even more compromises were necessary once the Constitution was revealed to the public. People in some states thought too many powers had been given to the federal government. In other states, people thought that important federal powers had been left out.

Read Chapter 79, pages 375–377. Be prepared to discuss the arguments made for and against acceptance of this new Constitution. Write a brief definition for the following term in your History Journal—*ratify*.

Name _____     Date _____

## Understanding the Preamble

Fill in the six purposes of the Constitution as outlined in the Preamble. Then define each purpose in your own words and provide an example.

*We the People of the United States, in order to form a more perfect union, establish justice, ensure domestic tranquility, provide for the common defense, promote the general welfare, and secure the blessings of liberty to ourselves and our posterity, do ordain and establish this Constitution for the United States of America.*

| List the goals set in the Preamble. | Explain each goal in your own words. | Provide an example. |
| --- | --- | --- |
| | | |
| | | |
| | | |
| | | |
| | | |
| | | |
| | | |

# Student Guide
## Lesson 7: Ratification!

After a long, hot summer of secrecy, arguments, threats, and compromise, the delegates finally presented a Constitution to the states for ratification. Now it was each state's turn to compromise—in order to create "a more perfect union."

### Lesson Objectives

- List the major supporters and opponents of ratification in 1787.
- Summarize the arguments for and against the ratification of the Constitution.
- Recognize the difficulties faced by delegates to the Constitutional Convention.
- State the six purposes of the Constitution found in the Preamble.
- Distinguish between the Declaration of Independence and the Constitution.
- Explain that the reason for calling the convention in Philadelphia was the need to revise the Articles of Confederation or write a new Constitution.
- Recognize the arguments for and against keeping the convention debates a secret.
- Identify Roger Sherman as the delegate who proposed the compromise we use today.
- Explain the Virginia Plan and the New Jersey Plan in terms of representation.

## PREPARE

Approximate lesson time is 60 minutes.

### Materials

For the Student

A History of US (Concise Edition), Volume A (Prehistory to 1800) by Joy Hakim

History Journal

## LEARN
### Activity 1: For and Against (Offline)
#### Instructions
#### Check Your Reading (Chapter 79, pages 375–377)

Review Chapter 79. Answer the following question to review your reading: Why did some people oppose the Constitution?

#### Use What You Know

In your History Journal, make a chart or list showing who supported and who opposed ratification and why.

Now take on the role of a delegate. Using the information in your chart, deliver a brief speech in which you argue for or against ratification of the Constitution. Explain the difficulty you have had reaching your decision.

**Look Back**

- Review Unit 7, Lessons 4–7 (Chapters 76–79).
- Review vocabulary words, writing, and worksheets in your History Journal.
- Go online and review the Constitutional Convention Flash Cards.

## ASSESS

### Mid-Unit Assessment: Ratification! (*Online*)

You will complete an online Mid-Unit Assessment covering the main goals for Lessons 4, 5, 6, and 7. Your assessment will be scored by the computer.

# Student Guide
## Lesson 8. Optional: Mason Makes His Mark

George Mason was a Virginia delegate who helped form Virginia's government, drafting the Virginia Declaration of Rights and the Virginia State Constitution. Mason was concerned primarily with preserving individual rights and was an adamant supporter of the Bill of Rights.

Even though you may skip this lesson, you must complete the **Read On** activity before moving on to the next lesson.

### Lesson Objectives
- Demonstrate knowledge gained in previous lessons.
- Use the Internet to gain information on George Mason.
- Evaluate Mason's contributions to the United States as the chief supporter of the Bill of Rights.

---

# PREPARE

Approximate lesson time is 60 minutes.

### Materials
> For the Student
>> A History of US (Concise Edition), Volume A (Prehistory to 1800) by Joy Hakim
>> History Journal

---

# LEARN
## Activity 1. Optional: George Mason *(Offline)*
### Instructions
**Use What You Know**

Visit the Gunston Hall website and click "George Mason On-Line" to learn about George Mason and the Constitution. After you explore the site, list three things in your History Journal that you learned about George Mason and his thoughts about the Bill of Rights.

**Read On**

The delegates who wrote the Constitution intended it to be the supreme law of the land. They also made sure that no part of the government got too powerful. The Constitution is a beautiful document that is written simply, clearly, and very carefully. The Framers provided a way to change it, but they didn't make it easy. Read Chapter 80, pages 378–383. Be prepared to discuss the duties of each of the three branches of government, and to find current newspaper or magazine articles that demonstrate the powers and duties of those three branches.

---

Vocabulary

You'll see these terms as you read. Write a brief definition for each term in your History Journal.

- checks and balances
- amendment

# Student Guide
## Lesson 9: The Constitution: Branches and Balances

The Constitution is alive and well today as the supreme law of the United States of America. We still have three separate, balanced branches of government—each with the power to check one another. You won't have to look hard to find current events that either challenge the Constitution or turn to it for guidance.

### Lesson Objectives
- Identify the Constitution as the supreme law of the land.
- Identify the three branches of government and summarize the role of each branch, including the concept of checks and balances.
- Define *amendment* and explain the purpose of amendments.

## PREPARE

Approximate lesson time is 60 minutes.

### Materials
> For the Student
>> 🖳 Constitutional Branches and Balances
>>
>> A History of US (Concise Edition), Volume A (Prehistory to 1800) by Joy Hakim
>>
>> History Journal

## LEARN
### Activity 1: A Good Constitution Endures *(Offline)*
#### Instructions
#### Check Your Reading (Chapter 80, pages 378–383)

- Go over Chapter 80.
- Complete the Constitutional Branches and Balances sheet.
- Check your answers with an adult.

**Use What You Know**

People use and challenge the Constitution all the time. Newspapers often have articles that demonstrate the powers of the three branches of government. With an adult, review recent newspapers or go online to a major newspaper to find examples of checks and balances in government action. Here are some examples you are likely to find:

- Congress (the legislature) reviews executive or judicial nominations (for example, a cabinet official or a federal judge).
- The Courts (judicial) review executive actions or congressional legislation (for example, ruling a law or executive action unconstitutional).

- Congress approves executive actions in foreign policy (treaties or military activity).
- Executive approves or vetoes congressional legislation.
- State and federal governments share (and sometimes argue over) powers regarding issues such as education or roads.

Identify one or more issues. Then, in your History Journal, write a brief summary of one issue. Identify the branches of government involved, and describe their roles in terms of checks and balances.

Name _____    Date _____

## Constitutional Branches and Balances

You'll find the answers to these questions in Chapter 80. Write your answers in the spaces provided.

1. The Constitution is law, but it is no ordinary law. Explain the difference between the Constitution and legislation.

    _____

    _____

    _____

2. According to the author, what has helped make the Constitution long lasting?

    _____

3. What is one of the first things the delegates to the Constitutional Convention decided on?

    _____

4. James Madison's Virginia Plan called for three branches of government. The delegates agreed to build this into the Constitution. Identify the three branches, and write a brief summary of the role each branch plays in government.

    _____

    _____

    _____

5. The delegates were afraid of power. They had already divided the government into three branches. What do we call the system they used to make sure that no one branch of the government gets too much power over the other branches? Can you give one example of this system in practice? Which branches does it involve?

    _____

    _____

    _____

    _____

**6.** What are two things that all the delegates agreed they wanted in the Constitution?

_____

_____

_____

**7.** What are the two ways the delegates solved the problem of power?

_____

_____

_____

**8.** Which part of the government, if any, is allowed to break the rules of the Constitution?

_____

**9.** What is the term for changes to the Constitution? Describe what must happen for a constitutional change to be accepted.

_____

_____

_____

_____

**10.** To date, about how many changes have been suggested for the Constitution? How many have been accepted?

_____

# Student Guide
## Lesson 10: The Constitution: What Does It Say?

One of the nice things about the U.S. Constitution is that it is not very complicated. If you read it carefully, you will understand it. It is that simplicity that has helped make the Constitution so lasting.

### Lesson Objectives
- Analyze the Constitution to gain familiarity with its structure.

# PREPARE

Approximate lesson time is 60 minutes.

### Materials
For the Student

💻 Constitutional Scavenger Hunt

A History of US (Concise Edition), Volume A (Prehistory to 1800) by Joy Hakim

History Journal

# LEARN
## Activity 1: Getting into the Constitution *(Offline)*
### Instructions
#### Discuss

The Constitution is made up of a preamble followed by seven articles. How are these two parts different? What is the purpose of the preamble, and what is the purpose of the rest of the document?

#### Use What You Know

The Constitution is a well-organized document that is not hard to read. Get ready to roll up your sleeves and take a good look at it as you try to find the answers to the Constitutional Scavenger Hunt.

- Discuss with an adult the word *clause* and how it relates to the Constitution.
- Print the Constitutional Scavenger Hunt sheet and follow the instructions.

#### Read On

The Constitution defined a powerful new federal government. But what about the rights of individual citizens and of the states? The Constitution didn't say much about the freedoms, rights, protections, and powers that the people and the states felt they needed to "secure the blessings of liberty." For this, they needed a Bill of Rights.

Read Chapter 81, pages 384–388. Be prepared to identify the kinds of rights that are protected by the Bill of Rights. Also be prepared to discuss the rights and responsibilities of citizenship in a republic.

Vocabulary

Write a brief definition of the following terms:

- Bill of Rights
- republic

**Optional: Beyond the Lesson**

Go online to learn more about the U.S. Constitution.

# Activity 2. Optional: The Constitution: What Does It Say? *(Online)*

Name _____     Date _____

## Constitutional Scavenger Hunt

The text of the United States Constitution is located at the back of your book. You can find the answers to these questions there. Answer the questions aloud or in writing. Work with an adult. When you think you've got the answer to a question, check with an adult. Ask for help if you get stuck. After you answer a question correctly, place a check next to that number and move on to the next one. Good luck, and have fun!

1. Article I gives legislative, or lawmaking, power to _____. Article II gives the president _____ power. Article III gives judicial power to _____ and to inferior (lower) courts.

2. Which article of the Constitution addresses the rights of the states?

3. Which article of the Constitution addresses how the Constitution can be amended?

4. Article VI, clause (paragraph) 2, states that judges in every state must go by what the Constitution says. It says that the Constitution is the _____ of the land.

5. How many of the 13 states were required to ratify the Constitution before it could go into effect? (Look in the last article of the Constitution.)

Now go back to Article I to find out more about Congress.

6. How old would you have to be to serve in the House of Representatives?

7. To impeach means to formally accuse an official of a crime. Who has the "sole power of impeachment" in the Constitution?

8. How many senators are there from each state?

9. What is the term (number of years) served by a member of the Senate?

10. What is the minimum age for a senator?

11. Only one constitutional responsibility is defined for the vice president. What is it?

Now take a closer look at the executive branch in Article II.

12. What is the minimum age for a president?

**13.** What oath must the president-elect take before assuming the office of the presidency?

**14.** Article II, Section 2, clause 2, identifies two powers of the president. What are those powers? (This clause also identifies congressional checks on those powers.)

Find out more about Article III.

**15.** The only crime defined by the Constitution can be found in Article III, Section 3. What is it? Article IV, you remember, deals with the states.

**16.** Which section of Article IV tells you that there could be 51 or 52 states someday?

Look at Article V to find out how things change.

**17.** If two-thirds of the Congress or two-thirds of the states propose an amendment to the

Constitution, it will take effect when _____ of the states ratify it.

# Student Guide
## Lesson 11: The Bill of Rights

As soon as Americans saw the newly written Constitution, they set out to improve it. They wanted a bill of rights. Some states proposed amendments as they voted to ratify the Constitution. Then James Madison wrote the amendments we call the Bill of Rights. These first 10 amendments to the Constitution still protect Americans' freedom today.

### Lesson Objectives
- Demonstrate knowledge gained in previous lessons.
- Identify the major rights guaranteed by the Bill of Rights.
- Discuss the responsibilities of citizens in maintaining democracy.
- State the six purposes of the Constitution found in the Preamble.
- Identify the Constitution as the supreme law of the land.
- Identify the three branches of government and summarize the role of each branch, including the concept of checks and balances.
- Define *amendment* and explain the purpose of amendments.

# PREPARE

Approximate lesson time is 60 minutes.

### Materials
For the Student
- Cover Me, Bill of Rights!
- A History of US (Concise Edition), Volume A (Prehistory to 1800) by Joy Hakim
- History Journal
- The Bill of Rights Assessment Sheet

# LEARN
## Activity 1: "To Secure the Blessings of Liberty" *(Offline)*
### Instructions
**Check Your Reading (Chapter 81, pages 384–388)**

Review Chapter 81 by discussing the following with an adult:

1. Why didn't the Framers include a bill of rights in the original Constitution?
2. The Bill of Rights defines many of the rights of citizens. However, with rights come responsibilities. What are the responsibilities of the citizens of a democratic republic?
3. How do many of the rights defined in the Bill of Rights promote responsible citizenship?

## Use What You Know

- With an adult, read the Bill of Rights located at the back of the book.
- Complete the Cover Me, Bill of Rights! sheet. Identify which amendment protects you in each of the situations described.
- Check your answers with an adult.

## Review

Review online with the flash cards. (Hint: If you can correctly answer all of the questions on the flash cards, you'll do great on the assessment!)

# ASSESS
## Mid-Unit Assessment: The Bill of Rights (*Offline*)

You will complete an offline Mid-Unit Assessment covering the main goals for Lessons 9, 10, and 11. An adult will score the assessment and enter the results online.

Name _____     Date _____

## Cover Me, Bill of Rights!

The Bill of Rights is "insurance" that covers you in the form of rights and protections from government abuse. The situations presented here are made up. For each situation, review the explanation of the Bill of Rights in the book, and identify which amendment is involved. You will have to use the Bill of Rights at the back of the book to answer the last two questions. Write the amendment number and which right or protection applies in the spaces provided.

1. You have been arrested for a crime. At your trial, you are forced to answer questions, even though you don't want to.

   Amendment: _____ Right or protection: _____

   _____

2. A local army base doesn't have housing for all its soldiers. You're ordered to provide a room, bed, shower, laundry, and meals for a soldier in your home.

   Amendment: _____ Right or protection: _____

   _____

3. The government establishes an official religion and bans all other religions.

   Amendment: _____ Right or protection: _____

   _____

4. A crime is committed at your workplace. When you get home, you learn the police searched your home and seized your computer while you weren't there.

   Amendment: _____ Right or protection: _____

   _____

5. The government decides that a particular state or any citizen of that state may not own firearms.

   Amendment: _____ Right or protection: _____

   _____

6. The government decides that newspapers and book and magazine publishers can't print any writings that aren't in line with the government's views.

   Amendment: _____ Right or protection: _____

   _____

7. You are caught stealing a car, tried, and convicted. You are fined ten million dollars and sentenced to life in solitary confinement.

   Amendment: _____ Right or protection: _____

   _____

8. You are arrested for stealing a new car. The judge does not allow you to have a trial by jury.

   Amendment: _____ Right or protection: _____

   _____

Name _____ Date _____

# Mid-Unit Assessment

1. The Fourth, Fifth, Sixth, Seventh, and Eighth Amendments guarantee the rights and

   protections that would give an accused person a fair _____.

2. What are three freedoms guaranteed by the First Amendment?

   _____

   _____

   _____

3. What do we call the system devised by the Framers of the Constitution that prevents any
   one branch of government from gaining too much power over any other branch?

   _____

4. What is another name for the first 10 amendments to the Constitution?

   _____

5. In which branch of the government would you find the president, who enforces laws?

   _____

6. In which branch of the government would you find Congress, which creates laws?

   _____

7. Why is it important to be able to amend the Constitution?

   _____

   _____

   _____

8. The Constitution cannot be overruled by any state or law. It is the _____
   of the land.

**9.** What do we call a change to the Constitution? _____

**10.** In which branch of the government would you find the Supreme Court, which interprets laws, or decides their meaning? _____

**11.** What is the preamble to the Constitution?

_____

_____

# *Student Guide*
## Lesson 12: Unit Review

You've completed Unit 7, The Constitution. It's time to review what you've learned. You'll take the Unit Assessment in the next lesson.

### Lesson Objectives

- Review important knowledge and skills taught in this unit.

# PREPARE

Approximate lesson time is 60 minutes.

### Materials

For the Student

A History of US (Concise Edition), Volume A (Prehistory to 1800) by Joy Hakim

History Journal

# LEARN
## Activity 1: A Look Back *(Offline)*
### Instructions
### Online Review

Go online and use the following to review this unit:

- The Big Picture
- Time Line
- Flash Cards

### History Journal Review

Review some more by going through your History Journal. Look at the worksheets you completed for this unit. Review your vocabulary words. If you completed any writing assignments, read them. Don't rush through; take your time. Your History Journal is a great resource for a unit review.

# *Student Guide*
## Lesson 13: Unit Assessment

You've finished this unit! Now take the Unit Assessment.

### Lesson Objectives

- Demonstrate mastery of important knowledge and skills in this unit.
- Explain the need for and significance of state constitutions during the Revolution.
- Explain the importance of the Northwest Ordinance in terms of future territories and the precedents it set for education and slavery.
- Summarize the arguments for and against the ratification of the Constitution.
- Identify the three branches of government and summarize the role of each branch, including the concept of checks and balances.
- Define *amendment* and explain the purpose of amendments.
- Identify the major rights guaranteed by the Bill of Rights.
- Identify James Madison as the man given the title "Father of the Constitution."
- Explain that the reason for calling the convention in Philadelphia was the need to revise the Articles of Confederation or write a new Constitution.
- Summarize the issues on which the delegates to the Constitutional Convention were divided, including representation and slavery.
- Evaluate Mason's contributions to the United States as the chief supporter of the Bill of Rights.

---

# PREPARE

Approximate lesson time is 60 minutes.

### Materials

For the Student

    📠 The Constitution Assessment Sheet

---

# ASSESS

## Unit Assessment: The Constitution (*Offline*)

Complete the offline Unit Assessment. Your Learning Coach will score it and enter the results online.

---

Name _____     Date _____

# Unit Assessment

1. Match each term on the left with a description on the right. Write the correct letter on the blank line. There is one extra description on the right that does not match any of the terms on the left.

_____ Separation of powers

_____ Articles of Confederation

_____ Checks and balances

_____ Connecticut Compromise

_____ The Bill of Rights

_____ Preamble

_____ The Virginia Plan

_____ The Constitution

A. The statement of the six purposes for the Constitution

B. Equal representation in the legislature

C. The first 10 amendments to the Constitution

D. The division of political power among branches of government

E. Representation in the legislature based on population

F. The system that prevents any one branch of the government from gaining too much power over the other branches

G. The supreme law of the land

H. The first government of the United States

I. A plan for a two-house legislature based on population in one house and equal representation in the other

2. Match each person on the left with the description on the right. Write the correct letter on the blank line. There is one extra description that does not match any of the people on the left.

_____ James Madison

_____ Alexander Hamilton

_____ George Mason

A. The delegate to the Constitutional Convention who proposed the Great Compromise

B. The Father of the Constitution

C. A Virginian who refused to sign the Constitution, but was the chief supporter of the Bill of Rights

D. The New York delegate to the Constitutional Convention who wrote most of the Federalist Papers in support of the Constitution

3. Which of the following is **NOT** a reason that the Northwest Ordinance was important?

   (A) It provided a way for territories to organize and enter the union as states.

   (B) It encouraged explorers to find a northwest passage to the Pacific.

   (C) It encouraged education and provided a way for public schools to be supported.

   (D) It prohibited slavery in the Northwest Territory.

4. The Constitutional Convention was held because _____.

   (A) James Madison wanted to keep and improve the Articles of Confederation

   (B) the Northwest Territory wanted to draft a state constitution and become a new state

   (C) the weak government under the Articles of Confederation, which had no power to tax, needed to be revised or replaced

   (D) Virginia, New Jersey, and Connecticut all wanted their state constitutions to become the United States Constitution

5. Why is it important to be able to amend the Constitution?

   (A) Amendments allow us to improve the Constitution over time.

   (B) The Constitution is a set of super laws that cannot be changed.

   (C) The paper it is written on is old and falling apart and needs to be restored from time to time.

   (D) New presidents need to be able to make the changes that they want.

6. In the space provided, number each of the four documents in the order in which they were written, with 1 being first and 4 being last.

   _____ The Articles of Confederation

   _____ The Bill of Rights

   _____ The Declaration of Independence

   _____ The Constitution

Write your answers to these questions in complete sentences.

7. After the states had driven the British colonial governments out, it was important for them to create state constitutions. How did this help in writing the U.S. Constitution?

_____

_____

_____

8. What are two of the major issues that divided the Constitutional Convention on which the delegates had to compromise?

_____

_____

_____

9. The Constitution is made up of a preamble followed by seven articles. How are these two parts different?

_____

_____

_____

10. Write the letter for each of the following arguments for and against ratification of the Constitution in the appropriate column.

   **A.** Individual liberties are protected under the Constitution.

   **B.** The Constitution does not include a bill of rights.

   **C.** The states have to give up power to the federal government under the Constitution.

   **D.** The Constitution creates a strong national government.

   **E.** Slavery is still allowed under the Constitution.

   **F.** George Washington approves of the Constitution.

| **For Ratification** | **Against Ratification** |
|:---:|:---:|
| _____ | _____ |
| _____ | _____ |
| _____ | _____ |

**11.** The U.S. government is divided into three branches. In the spaces below, fill in the name of each branch, the person or group in that branch, and the major job of each group. One answer for each group is already provided.

Name of branch     <u>legislative</u>    _____    _____

Headed up by     _____    President    _____

What it does     _____    _____    Rules on laws

**12.** Identify three First Amendment freedoms guaranteed in the Bill of Rights.

_____

_____

**13.** In the Bill of Rights, the Fourth, Fifth, Sixth, Seventh, and Eighth Amendments to the Constitution guarantee the rights and protections that would give an accused person a

_____ trial.

# *Student Guide*
## Lesson 14: Semester Review

You've completed the first semester. It's time to review what you've learned.

The next two lessons are optional and can be used to further review for the Semester Assessment.

### Lesson Objectives
- Prepare for the assessment by reviewing content and skills presented in this semester.

---

# PREPARE

Approximate lesson time is 60 minutes.

### Materials
    For the Student
        A History of US (Concise Edition), Volume A (Prehistory to 1800) by Joy Hakim
        History Journal

---

# LEARN
## Activity 1: A Look Back *(Offline)*
### Instructions
### History Journal Review

Review the first semester by going through your History Journal. You should review:

- Completed work
- Maps
- Vocabulary
- Assessments

### Online Review

Go online and use the following to review the first semester:

- Flash cards
- Big Pictures

---

The following Unit Review lessons have a Big Picture:

- Unit 1, Lesson 11
- Unit 2, Lesson 10
- Unit 3, Lesson 9
- Unit 4, Lesson 12
- Unit 5, Lesson 14
- Unit 6, Lesson 8
- Unit 7, Lesson 12

As you review the Big Pictures, write an assessment item for each unit that you think should be included on the first semester assessment. You can use multiple choice, fill-in-the-blank, and matching. Include the correct answer.

Do this work on notebook paper. Have an adult check your work, and then put it in your History Journal.

# Student Guide
## Lesson 15: (Optional) Semester Review

Use this OPTIONAL lesson to prepare for the Semester Assessment.

### Lesson Objectives
- Prepare for the assessment by reviewing content and skills presented in this semester.

---

# PREPARE

Approximate lesson time is 60 minutes.

# Student Guide
## Lesson 16: (Optional) Semester Review

Use this OPTIONAL lesson to prepare for the Semester Assessment.

### Lesson Objectives
- Prepare for the assessment by reviewing content and skills presented in this semester.

---

## PREPARE

Approximate lesson time is 60 minutes.

---

# Student Guide
## Lesson 17: Semester Assessment

You have finished the first semester. Take the Semester Assessment. Then prepare for the next lesson.

## Lesson Objectives

- Demonstrate mastery of important knowledge and skills in this unit.
- Identify geographic reasons for diversity among Native American groups.
- Explain the reasons for European desire to go to Asia, including an interest in learning and the desire for power, wealth, and goods.
- Explain the reason for the introduction of African slavery into the Americas as a way to fill the need for field workers.
- Explain the causes of the French and Indian War as competition between France and England for land and power.
- Identify and describe the Stamp Act.
- Explain the importance of the Northwest Ordinance in terms of future territories and the precedents it set for education and slavery.
- Identify the three branches of government and summarize the role of each branch, including the concept of checks and balances.
- Identify the major rights guaranteed by the Bill of Rights.
- Describe three changes that occurred as a result of the Spanish introduction of the horse to North America.
- Identify the House of Burgesses as the first representative assembly in the European colonies.
- Describe the factors in England that pushed people to come to America, including poverty and a growing population.
- Explain the reasons for conflict between English settlers and Native Americans as racism and the disagreement over land use and ownership.
- Identify James Madison as the man given the title "Father of the Constitution."

---

# PREPARE

Approximate lesson time is 60 minutes.

## Materials

For the Student

📖 American History A, Semester 1 Assessment Sheet

📖 George Washington

A History of US (Concise Edition), Volume B (1790-1877) by Joy Hakim

History Journal

---

# ASSESS
## Semester Assessment: American History A, Semester 1 (*Offline*)
Complete the offline Semester Assessment. Your Learning Coach will score it and enter the results online.

# LEARN
## Activity 1: Chapters 1 and 2 (*Offline*)
### Instructions
### Read On

The new Constitution called for an elected president. Do you know who the first president was? He was also called "the father of our country." His name is George Washington, and he was an impressive man. He left his beloved home to serve his country as the first president in 1789. No one had been president before, so he had a lot to do. You will read about some of the things he did as the nation was just beginning.

Read Chapter 1, pages 2–5, and Chapter 2, pages 6–8, in *A History of US (Concise Edition),* Volume B (1790-1877). Complete the "What I Know" and "What I Want to Know" columns of the George Washington sheet. Review your answers with an adult.

Name _____       Date _____

## George Washington

Think about what you already know and what you want to
know about George Washington. Complete the first two
columns of the chart below. Then read Chapter 1 in *A History
of US (Concise Edition)*, Volume B. After you finish reading,
complete the last column.

| What I Know | What I Wanted to Know | What I Learned |
|---|---|---|
|  |  |  |

Name                                            Date

## Semester Assessment

1. The introduction of the _____ to North America drastically changed the lives of many American Indians.

   (A) mule

   (B) chicken

   (C) horse

   (D) turkey

2. Which of the following had the biggest effect on the way in which Native American culture groups developed?

   (A) the time period in which they settled an area

   (B) the geography and climate of the area they settled

   (C) the kind of writing and language the group used

   (D) the ability of the group to use animals for farming

3. African slavery was introduced to the Americas because:

   (A) It could fill the large need for workers on sugar plantations.

   (B) The Spanish conquered Africa and took millions of Africans as slaves.

   (C) The Spanish needed a large army to defeat the Native Americans, and African slaves were immune to New World diseases.

   (D) A potato famine in Africa forced millions of starving Africans into slavery.

4. Why were fifteenth-century Europeans so eager to find a sea route to East Asia?

   (A) Spanish explorers wanted to find a way to sail around the world.

   (B) They wanted to quickly and easily send emigrants to the Indies.

   (C) They wanted an easier, shorter way to the riches of the Indies.

   (D) Inhabitants of China, Japan, and India were eager to travel to Europe.

5. Which of the following was among the biggest factors that determined how people lived and worked in the American colonies?

   Ⓐ education and money

   Ⓑ background and skills

   Ⓒ personality and character

   Ⓓ geography and climate

6. What were the two main factors that caused large numbers of people to leave England and go to America?

   Ⓐ widespread poverty and a growing population in England

   Ⓑ desire for adventure and interest in exploration among English farm workers

   Ⓒ growing upper class and a dwindling population in the Americas

   Ⓓ interest in getting rich quick and escaping arrest

7. What was the main reason for the problems that existed between Native Americans and the English colonists in North America?

   Ⓐ inability to communicate with each other

   Ⓑ different beliefs about the ownership and use of the land

   Ⓒ differences in religious beliefs and ideas of morality

   Ⓓ use of slaves by Indians while colonists believed slavery was wrong

8. What was the main cause of the French and Indian War?

   Ⓐ disagreements between England and its colonies over taxation

   Ⓑ westward migration of colonists into the Ohio Valley

   Ⓒ competition between France and England for land and power

   Ⓓ destruction of Indian villages by French and English settlers

9. Why did England enact the Stamp Act?

   (A) England needed to raise money for a war it was fighting with Spain.

   (B) England needed to raise money to pay off debts after the French and Indian War.

   (C) England wanted its colonies to be poor so that they could not rebel.

   (D) England wanted the colonists to make their own paper goods in order to reduce their costs.

10. Which country's contributions helped the Americans win the Revolutionary War?

    (A) Spain

    (B) Portugal

    (C) Holland

    (D) France

11. Which of the following was an important part of the Northwest Ordinance?

    (A) It required that townships set aside land for public schools.

    (B) It allowed slavery and involuntary servitude.

    (C) It included a system for dividing land into areas called states.

    (D) It prohibited the practice of religion and trial by jury.

12. Which of the following was one of the first experiments in self-government in England's American colonies?

    (A) Article of Confederation

    (B) House of Burgesses

    (C) Constitutional Convention

    (D) Second Continental Congress

13. Who is referred to as the Father of the Constitution?

    (A) George Washington

    (B) Thomas Jefferson

    (C) James Madison

    (D) Alexander Hamilton

**14.** Which of the following best summarizes the Bill of Rights?

Ⓐ laws which guarantee the rights of states

Ⓑ demands for payment for the rights of indentured servants

Ⓒ amendments to the Constitution that guarantee individual rights and state powers

Ⓓ the right of Congress to amend the U.S. Constitution

**15.** What are the three branches of government?

Ⓐ Legislative, Congress, Executive

Ⓑ President, Judicial, Legislative

Ⓒ Executive, Supreme Court, Congress

Ⓓ Legislative, Executive, Judicial

*(4 points)*
**16.** Match each group of people on the left with the phrase on the right that best describes the group. There is one phrase on the right that does not match any group on the left.

_____ George Washington, Marquis de Lafayette, Lord Charles Cornwallis, and George Rogers Clark

**A.** These men were all U.S. presidents.

**B.** These men were founders and leaders of some of the colonies.

_____ Patrick Henry, Sam Adams, and Thomas Paine

**C.** These men were among the First American authors.

_____ Roger Williams, James Oglethorpe, and William Penn

**D.** These men were patriots who helped spark a revolution.

_____ Thomas Jefferson, James Madison, George Washington

**E.** These men were military leaders during the Revolutionary War.

**(7 points)**

**17.** Place the following events on the time line below in the order in which they occurred.

    **A.** Americans defeat British forces at Yorktown with help from France.

    **B.** Jamestown is founded as an English colony in Virginia.

    **C.** People migrate over Berengia into North America.

    **D.** Rhode Island becomes the 13th state to ratify the U.S. Constitution.

    **E.** The Spanish conquest destroys the Aztec civilization.

    **F.** The Declaration of Independence is signed in Philadelphia.

    **G.** The colonies of Maryland, Pennsylvania, and Rhode Island are founded.

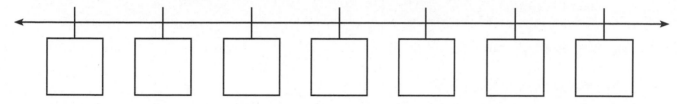

**(3 points)**

**18.** Label this map to show the general areas in which the following nations focused their explorations. Write the letter of each country in the square where it belongs.

    **A.** England

    **B.** France

    **C.** Spain

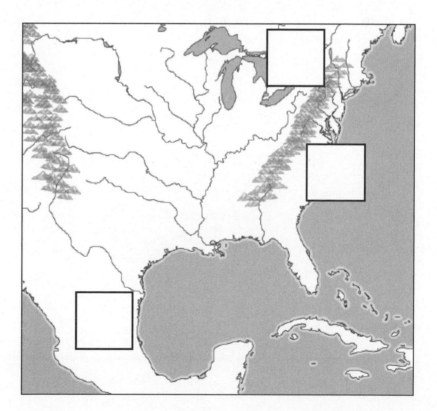

**(6 points)**

**19.** Sequence the following documents in the order in which they were written by numbering them 1–6. Number 1 should be the first document to be written and number 6 should be the last.

_____ U.S. Constitution

_____ Articles of Confederation

_____ Magna Carta

_____ Bill of Rights

_____ Mayflower Compact

_____ Declaration of Independence